Brand You

Turn your unique talents into a
winning formula

second edition

**John Purkiss
and
David Royston-Lee**

Harlow, England • London • New York • Boston • San Francisco • Toronto • Sydney • Auckland • Singapore • Hong Kong
Tokyo • Seoul • Taipei • New Delhi • Cape Town • São Paulo • Mexico City • Madrid • Amsterdam • Munich • Paris • Milan

PEARSON EDUCATION LIMITED

Edinburgh Gate
Harlow CM20 2JE
Tel: +44 (0)1279 623623
Fax: +44 (0)1279 431059
Website: www.pearson.com/uk

First published by Artesian Publishing LLP in 2009
Second edition published by Pearson Education Limited 2012 (print and electronic)

© John Purkiss and David Royston-Lee 2012 (print and electronic)

The rights of John Purkiss and David Royston-Lee to be identified as authors of this work
have been asserted by them in accordance with the Copyright, Designs and Patents Act 1988.

Pearson Education is not responsible for the content of third-party internet sites.

ISBN: 978-0-273-77769-4 (print)
      978-0-273-77920-9 (PDF)
      978-0-273-77921-6 (ePub)
      978-0-273-77919-3 (eText)

British Library Cataloguing-in-Publication Data
A catalogue record for this book is available from the British Library

Library of Congress Cataloging-in-Publication Data
A catalog record for this book is available from the Library of Congress

10 9 8 7 6 5 4
16

Cover designed by David Carroll & Co
Typeset in 10/15pt ITC Giovanni Std by 3
Printed and bound in Great Britain by Henry Ling Limited, at the Dorset Press,
Dorchester, DT1 1HD

NOTE THAT ANY PAGE CROSS REFERENCES REFER TO THE PRINT EDITION

'Original insights in a concise format – *Brand You* is an inspiring read.'

BB Cooper, composer

'This is a really important book to help you discover your uniqueness and how that contributes to the world.'

Nick Williams, author of The Work You Were Born to Do *and co-founder of inspired-entrepreneur.com*

'Not only does this book set the context for why personal brand-building is more important than ever. It also has well-structured, insightful and practical words on what to do about it.'

Theresa Wise, founder, T Wise Consulting

'*Brand You* is a great book that reflects the age where, to be your best, you need to have a personal brand. If you want to be the first choice on people's list of business contacts, then read *Brand You*.'

Peter Cook, author of Sex, Leadership and Rock'n'Roll *and* Best Practice Creativity

'People often don't think enough about the impact they have on others, and how they are perceived. This book shows you how to ensure that people's perception of you fits reality. You will have far more impact, which will help you to build a successful career.'

Amanda Alexander, partner, Stork & May

'A refreshing, insightful and practical guide to managing your most important product – you! Essential reading for anyone who wants to succeed.'

Ranjan Singh, internet entrepreneur, CEO of isango.com

'I was lucky enough to read this book just as I was rethinking my career. It proved invaluable.'

Kevin Mannion, social media consultant

'This is one of the most powerful books I have ever read. Its unique methodology works across all media – it will transform the profile of anyone who reads and applies it.'

Kully Dhadda, director, Flame Public Relations

'*Brand You* is easy to read and absorb. I was able to put the ideas into practice right away.'

Naazi Marouf, dentist

'*Brand You* helped me to position myself with the press and donors. Remarkable stuff.'

Dr Eben Upton, founder, The Raspberry Pi Foundation

Brand You

For Maureen, Alice, Theo and Jemima

Contents

Preface

You already have a brand. As Jeff Bezos, the founder of Amazon, once said: 'Your brand is what people say about you when you are not in the room.' However, most people do little to *build* their brands. They get on with their work, hoping someone will notice them. They may be talented, but they are not well known. They have weak brands that hold them back. A strong brand will transform your career. This book will show you how to build it.

You may object that you are not a brand of soap powder or a soft drink, so the principles of marketing do not apply to you. That is certainly true among your family and close friends. They know and appreciate your many facets. However, other people spend far less time getting to know you. It is best to project a simple message that employers, clients and customers will remember. When they have a need, they will think of you.

We have developed a unique model that anyone can understand and apply. It will give you a deep understanding of who you are and what you do best. These are crucial steps. They will increase your energy and passion for your work – the key to a successful career. You will attract people who want what you have to offer.

We will show you how to develop a large, powerful web of relationships that brings you new opportunities and boosts your bank balance.

We strongly encourage you to complete the exercises. *Brand You* is like a guidebook to a distant country. While you are reading about it, you can experience it for yourself.

Acknowledgements

We would like to thank everyone who has contributed ideas, enthusiasm and constructive criticism: Amanda Alexander, Rose Alexander, Mohammad Al-Ubaydi, Dan Andrew, Sue Appleby, Abdul Rahman Azzam, David Badham, Fred Becker, Dr Irina Behnert, Dr James Bellini, Adam Bennett, Andy Black, Martin Bloom, Jo Bowlby, Christian Brensing, Anita Butt, Susan Cayley Pilkington, Chris Charlesworth, Gerry Cheung, Piotr Chmielewski, Semi Cho, Shin Yang Chuang, Corey Cook, Charles Cooper, Sara Cooper, Donato Cordeiro, Lincoln Coutts, Adam Coxen, Tom Daniel, Shelley Davies, Tony Dowd, Thomas Drewry, Richard Duvall, Dr Barbara Edlmair, Jackie Elton, James Essinger, Jude Flegel, Auriel Folkes, Andy Gannon, Tacis Gavoyannis, Zanna Gayle, Ozana Giusca, Karen Glossop, Shaun Gregory, Nick Grierson, Sanjaya Gunatilake, Julian Ha, David Harding, Caroline Hardwicke, Michael Hartz, Paul Haslam, Graham Hastie, Andy Hayward, Laura Heybrook, Graham Hill, Paul Hinder, Richard Hite, Gary Hughes, Hanadi Jabado, Bridget Jackson, Erica Judge, Lydia Kan, Martin Karlsson, Charles Kaye, Bali Kochar, Pallavi Kollareddy, Simon Laffin, Justin Lance, Max Landsberg, Shaun Lattin, Frank Lawrenson, Colin Lee, Natalia Leshchenko, Vito Levi D'Ancona, Russell Levinson, Mei Lin, David Lindsay, Bill Lucas, Sarah Lynch, Eric McClean, Teresa McCrone, Guy MacPherson-Grant, Kevin Mannion, Raine Marcus, Dr Naazi Marouf, Susan Mascarenhas, Martin Mason, Julie Meyer, Andy Milligan, Amanda Morris, Jamie Myatt, Aneta Nawojska, Safaa Nhairy, Janet O'Hehir, Emma Ormond, Mike O'Shea, Denise Parker, Barbara Paterson, Roger Pelliciotti, Anna Persin, Olga Petrovic, Mark Pilkington, Ric Piper, Jessica Pulay, Margaret Purkiss, Simon Purkiss, Stéphane Rambosson, Sirish Reddi, Ivna Reic, Mike Richards, Robin Rogers, Daniel Rogoff, Eric Rothbarth, Fraser

Runciman, Susanne Rutishauser, Joe Salem, Amanda Salmon, Laura Scaramella, Adam Selly, Harriet Sergeant, Sanjay Shah, Kerstin Shamma'a, Simon Silvester, Isabelle Smail, David Sparling, India Staunton, Andrei Stepanov, Cindy Stern, François Stieger, Valerie Stogdale, Xavier Szebrat, Dr Sándor Takács, Yasuhiko Takayanagi, Ting-Seng Tang, Yin Yin Tang, David Tarsh, Susan Tether, Tim Thimaya, Richard Thomas, Clifford Thurlow, Max Thurlow, Glenn Timms, Kahéna Tlili-Fitzgerald, Ted Townsend, Thuy Tran, Elisabeth Tschyrkow, Lawrence Tse, Bhav Ubi-Hull, Mohamed Uddin, Debra van Gene, Andrea von Finckenstein, Amanda Walker, Emily Landis Walker, Ashley Ward, Dave Watkin, Victoria Watson, John Williams, Gordon Willoughby, Charles Wilson, Susanne Worsfold, Clark Zhang and Suzan Ziobro.

We would like to thank and acknowledge those who have taught us, in particular Nella Barkley, Tony Bowley, Professor Ingemar Dierickx, David Fletcher, Sheldon Franklin, Sir John Hall, Barry Harrison, Professor Kevin Kingsland, Julia McCutchen, Barbara Minto, Dr Srikumar Rao, Mike Southon, Dr John Viney and Nick Williams. We would also like to thank Rose Alexander for her advice on legal issues, and Richard Thomas of Varihost (www.varihost.net) for his advice on websites, blogs and social media.

Publisher's acknowledgements

About the authors

John Purkiss studied economics at Cambridge University and has an MBA from INSEAD, where he was awarded the Henry Ford II Prize. Having spent his early career in banking and management consultancy, he has been an adviser to several high-growth companies. John was a partner with Heidrick & Struggles and now runs the leadership practice at Veni Partners. He is the co-author of *How to be Headhunted*. www.johnpurkiss.com

David Royston-Lee studied behavioural science at Aston University and occupational psychology at Birkbeck College, London. Having begun his career in recruitment, he became head of career management services at KPMG. David then worked as human resources director of Ogilvy & Mather. He was chief executive of the CAM Foundation prior to founding Partners in Flow. He is the author of *How to Win from the Start* and *The Career Repair Kit*. www.davidroystonlee.com

Chapter

1

Why build your brand?

Some people have never seen the need for personal marketing. They do their best at work and are promoted every now and again. However, the world has changed. The typical company man (literally) of the 1950s and 1960s spent his entire career with one or two organisations. Having completed his education and military service, he joined a company and progressed through the ranks. His job title told people what they needed to know about him.

In the West this model began to fall apart in the 1970s, when recession led to restructuring and a steep rise in unemployment. From the 1980s, cheap computing power eliminated the need for large numbers of middle managers. Since the early 1990s Eastern Europe and East Asia have embarked on a similar process. In Japan and South Korea, the children of those who worked for one company or the government are changing jobs more frequently. They may even start a business.

Another big change is the rising percentage of women in the workforce. In some countries, including the UK, more women than men now qualify in law and medicine each year. In Western Europe as a whole, women represent a small but steadily increasing percentage of board members of large companies.

So why exactly do you need to build your personal brand?

Give yourself greater flexibility in your career

Most of us spend our early years in a hierarchy: in our family, at school, at university and in our first jobs. Some employers offer excellent training and experience. However, the flatter an organisation becomes, the less likely it is to manage your career or keep you over the long term. As a result, you are likely to change jobs more frequently than your parents did. It is better to build your track record than to worry about hierarchies and internal politics. If someone fires you, someone else will want to hire you. It is more important to be employable than employed.

With the spread of broadband and mobile communications, we find ourselves in a global market. If face-to-face communication is not required, you can work or do business with almost anyone, anywhere. In the meantime the distinction between employment and self-employment has become blurred. More and more people move back and forth between the two. They train with one firm, join another, lose their job and then move to another sector. They take time out to study or have children. They move to another country and/or start a business. While all these changes are occurring, it is important to stay visible and attract the people who need your services. With the growth of the internet – and social media in particular – the ways of staying visible have multiplied.

Fifty years ago you might have been defined by your employer and your job title. People projected their employer's brand through their dress code, their habits of speech and the way they thought and behaved at work. Hence long-term employees of Procter & Gamble became *proctoids*. IBM, Pepsi and Shell had equally strong cultures. These cultures still exist, but people move in and out of them faster than before.

Instead of pursuing a traditional career, you can now tailor your work to your talents and interests. With less of a hierarchy to climb, you are more likely to move laterally, building your track record as you go. An IT specialist might implement the same software package for various organisations. A director of human resources might help to restructure one company after another. A chief executive might lead a series of companies in the same or related sectors.

Instead of relying on your current job title, it is better to convey exactly what you do, how you do it and how you want to develop from now on. This applies whether you are meeting people face to face or editing your profile on a website such as Google or LinkedIn. This book will help you do both.

Enhance your career prospects

Loyalty is less important than it was. Your employer is not a mother or father who will take care of you in good times and bad. Loyalty is unlikely to be rewarded with job security. Even blue-chip companies fire people who have spent decades working for them. They pay for performance, regardless of your job title. If you build a positive personal brand your employer will probably treat you well, in the hope that you will stay. You can move on whenever you want or need to.

While loyalty has declined, commitment remains essential. If you are employed, the best way to keep your job is to produce first-class work consistently. The same applies if you are self-employed. If you are known for excellence, clients will keep coming back to you.

Develop a portfolio career

Another trend is the growth in portfolio careers which combine activities. This is normal in the arts and the media. Leonardo da Vinci combined painting and drawing with designing tanks and helicopters. Comedians and sportspeople write books. Celebrities appear in TV commercials and play cameo roles in films. The portfolio approach has spread to other sectors. Some management consultants teach part-time at universities. We know a successful investor and company chairman who is also a professional photographer.

Some people want autonomy and a flexible lifestyle. Others work on several projects while they look for a new job. Technology has made portfolio careers much easier. Instead of going to the same office every day, you can use broadband and a mobile phone.

Women have pursued portfolio careers for centuries, combining childcare with part-time roles. For some this work is now highly paid. Penny Hughes became president of Coca-Cola UK & Ireland at the age of 33. She resigned two years later and has since been a non-executive director of The Body Shop, Next, Vodafone, Reuters, Gap, Skandinaviska Enskilda Banken, Cable & Wireless Worldwide and The Royal Bank of Scotland.

One of the UK's best-known portfolio non-executives is Allan Leighton. Since leading the successful turnaround of Asda – alongside the chairman, Archie Norman – he has been chairman or non-executive director of a wide range of companies, including Royal Mail, Lastminute.com, Bhs, Dyson, BSkyB, Leeds United Football Club and Selfridges.

Some companies prefer non-executives who work *full time* in a related field. For example, someone working in retail might sit on the board of a bank that wants to apply retail disciplines to its branch network.

The number of angel investors has also grown. Some have a full-time job but invest in a start-up company and sit on the board. Others devote most of their time to a portfolio of investments and directorships.

Make better use of your network

Your network is an important source of new opportunities. The older you are, the more likely you are to find your next job through personal contacts rather than through a recruitment firm. This is even true in sectors with plenty of specialist recruiters, such as finance and accountancy. In the UK, a survey of chartered accountants found that networking accounted for 20 per cent of successful job searches for people up to the age of 35; 80 per cent of them found a job through a recruitment firm. Between the ages of 35 and 50 the ratio was 50:50. For those older than 50, networking accounted for 80 per cent of all successful job searches.

Even if you are busy right now, it is worth keeping in touch with your network so that you hear of opportunities that might appeal to you.

It is easy to focus on the organisation that employs you and neglect your contacts elsewhere, while failing to develop new contacts. When you leave your current employer you will have to make a big effort to reconnect with other people. They may be understandably cynical when you suddenly get in touch with them after years of silence.

It does not have to be this way, particularly when you can use social networks such as LinkedIn and Google+ free of charge. Facebook is also beginning to support professional networking through applications such as BranchOut. These tools enable you to market yourself continuously, just as self-employed people and entrepreneurs do. This book will show you how.

Make sure you earn what you are worth

In most occupations lots of people have the skills required. But being good at what you do is not enough – you have to market yourself. If you produce first-class work, your boss or client will value you. However, they may still pay you below the market rate. If you make sure other people know what you can do, there will be several of them bidding for your services.

Think of a boss or client who rates you highly. What if you knew ten people like them – or a hundred? If more people knew about you, more of them would want to hire you. Your earnings would almost certainly rise. For this to happen, you need to appeal to a much wider audience.

Make it easier to market yourself

Most people probably realise that they need to market themselves. However, marketing does not mean sending out your CV to all and sundry. That makes you no different from any other job-seeker. As soon as you stop banging on doors, you will be largely forgotten. There is a difference between *marketing* and *selling*. This is how we define them:

- Marketing is building a relationship with your target audience, finding out their needs and telling them how you could meet those needs. It includes reaching out to new people as well as those you already know.
- Selling is the final stage in the marketing process. It is helping potential customers to make a decision. It is making sure you win a particular contract.

Some people try to sell themselves in the wrong way at the wrong time. You have probably heard them blow their own trumpets at meetings and social events. The same thing occurs online. They keep talking about themselves and their businesses in glowing terms. Unsurprisingly, other people 'unfriend' or 'unfollow' them. At the same time, both employers and headhunters receive CVs with long-winded introductions explaining how marvellous the author is. All of this is a big turn-off. Some people have the opposite problem. They are so terrified of selling themselves that they miss out on exciting opportunities.

The key is knowing *when* to sell yourself. There are times when you are expected to do so. You may be competing for a job or an assignment. It is late in the marketing process and you are already on the shortlist. Your potential employers or clients have invited you to make a presentation. They want to know why they should choose *you*.

How do you get on the shortlist? Other people's perceptions of you play a major role. They also determine the amount people will pay for your services. If you meet someone for the first time, it helps a lot if they have heard or read about you. You already have some credibility on which you can build. Ideally, people should experience you in three different ways, in different contexts. For example, they might hear about you, read about you and then meet you in person. They might see you on television or on a well-regarded website. They might be connected with you on Facebook or LinkedIn, in which case they could have been reading your posts for months. The more widely you are recognised, the greater will be the demand for your services. The most powerful endorsement is when you are recommended to a potential client or boss by someone they trust.

You have been marketing yourself since you were a small child, initiating and developing relationships. The same principles apply in your job or business. Most people prefer to work with those they know and trust. A relationship can last for years – maybe even a lifetime. Every now and then there will be an opportunity to work together.

Give yourself a competitive advantage

Personal branding is most developed in sectors where the rewards are high. These include the film industry, music and professional sport. Technology and social change have played a major role. There are now hundreds of TV channels, as well as DVDs and downloads. Film stars can reach a global audience through a variety of media formats. They are marketed worldwide, just like products, services and companies. In the meantime, the world's population has more than trebled from 2 billion in 1930 to 7 billion in 2011.

Musicians and sportspeople have also benefited. The launch of MTV in 1981 enabled singers such as Madonna and Cyndi Lauper to promote their music through video, while building a strong brand identity. In English professional football, the sale of the UK broadcasting rights to BSkyB pumped money into the Premier League, which became a showcase for players from all over the world. This enabled some footballers to earn significant salaries while endorsing a wide range of products. Here are some examples of strong personal brands, from a variety of sectors:

Acting:

George Clooney, Nicole Kidman, Penelope Cruz, Ewan McGregor

Architecture:

Norman Foster, Frank Gehry, I. M. Pei, Zaha Hadid, Renzo Piano

Business:

Richard Branson, Carlos Ghosn, Li Ka-shing, Nat Rothschild

Chefs:

Jamie Oliver, Nigella Lawson, Gordon Ramsay, Raymond Blanc

Classical music:

Thomas Adès, Philip Glass, Arvo Pärt, John Tavener

Fashion:

Georgio Armani, Tom Ford, Vivienne Westwood

Fiction:

Paulo Coelho, Milan Kundera, Doris Lessing, Salman Rushdie

Film-makers:

Pedro Almodóvar, Ridley Scott, Steven Spielberg, Martin Scorsese

Finance:

Prince Alwaleed Bin Talal, Warren Buffett, George Soros

Motor racing:

Bernie Ecclestone, Lewis Hamilton, Sebastian Vettel, Jenson Button

Painting:

David Hockney, Antoni Tàpies, Tracey Emin

Photography:

Araki, René Burri, Annie Leibovitz, Don McCullin, Steve McCurry

Politics:

Angela Merkel, Barack Obama, Wen Jiabao, Aung San Suu Kyi

Popular music:

Paul McCartney, Sting, Beyoncé, Rihanna, Lady Gaga

Royalty:

The Queen, William and Kate, Juan Carlos I of Spain, King Bhumibol of Thailand, Abdullah bin Abdul Aziz Al Saud

Sculpture:

Antony Gormley, Damien Hirst, Rachel Whiteread, Ai Weiwei

Sport:

David Beckham, Serena Williams, Rafael Nadal, Usain Bolt

Each has a following of millions of people. One reason is that the internet has made them more visible. Some have their own websites and Facebook pages. There are unofficial ones too, set up by fans or critics. If you want to know about any of these people, you can Google them in seconds.

Other occupations may be less visible to the general public. However, there are strong personal brands in every sector, including advertising, banking, consultancy, insurance, the law, medicine, public relations, consumer goods and manufacturing. Carlos Ghosn, a Brazilian of Lebanese descent, is chief executive of both Nissan and Renault. He built his early reputation in France, where he became known as *le cost killer.* If you type *le cost killer* into Google, there are millions of references to him, from all over the world. By any standard, that is a strong personal brand.

Business people deal with brands – their products, services and companies – every day, but often neglect their *personal* brands. However, in recent years top executives' earnings have grown much faster than average, bringing them closer to star performers in sport and the media. Some executives now hire consultants to market them to headhunters and potential employers. There are also public relations firms and advertising agencies that specialise in personal brands. Our own consultancy work in personal brand strategy began when people who had read the first edition of *Brand You* asked us to work with them.

A brand is an asset in its own right. Agencies such as Interbrand have developed valuation methods that they apply to brands ranging from Nike to Volkswagen. Increasingly, brands are being included as assets on companies' balance sheets. Likewise, your personal brand is an asset that can take on a life of its own. If you build it correctly, people will keep thinking and talking about you.

Your brand will bring you customers and revenues even when you are not working. Most of us do not need to be household names. It is enough to be well known among potential customers, clients, colleagues and suppliers, as well as to journalists and other commentators who follow your sector. Having defined your target audience, you can work out what you are going to do for them, and how you are going to tell them about it.

Find people who want what you offer

There are two main approaches to marketing, both of which have their uses. The first is to find out what people want and then develop a product or service that meets their needs. Many successful entrepreneurs are good at this. If their first customer is very demanding, so much the better! Once that customer is happy, the entrepreneur uses them as a reference when selling to others. This works with anything from sandwiches to software. It is the 'pull' approach to marketing.

The second approach is to develop a product or service and then find out who wants it. A famous example is the Post-It Note, invented by accident in 3M's laboratories. The company's researchers discovered a glue that could be applied to a sheet of paper but would not stick permanently to anything else. Likewise, when the personal computer was invented it was not obvious that large numbers of people would want one in their office, let alone at home or while they were travelling. However, the product was marketed effectively and became a worldwide success. This is the 'push' approach to marketing.

Something similar happens in advertising agencies. The client has a product or service – which may be new or decades old – and asks the agency to find ways of marketing it. The agency discovers new uses for the product, or variations that make it more attractive to more people. One example is Marmite, a savoury spread made from yeast extract, which has traditionally been sold in a glass jar. It is now available in an upside-down, 'squeezy' format. The brand has also been extended to Marmite-flavoured crisps (known in some countries as chips), which have enabled the brand to reach a new market.

Personal marketing has more in common with the second approach. The better you know yourself, the better you can market yourself. While you are growing up, you discover you are good at some things and not so good at others. You find some things exciting and others boring. We will start by helping you identify your *talents*. The second step is to discover your *values* – what you believe is important in your life and work. Then you can focus on what you love to do and do well. If you are true to your talents and your values, you will be *authentic*. You will naturally attract people – employers, customers and colleagues – who share some of your values and appreciate what you do best. Whether you are employed or self-employed, they will ask for you.

This does not mean that everyone will love you. Think of your favourite food. Some people love it, others cannot stand it. The same applies to you. Once you are clear about who you are and what you stand for, some people will flock to you; others will keep their distance. This makes it easier to find out who wants what you have to offer.

Instead of rushing around in search of your next piece of work, sit back for a while and think about your brand. How can you build it? The stronger your brand becomes, the more easily you will attract the work you want to do – and the rewards that go with it.

Chapter

2

How do brands work?

Brands in the broadest sense have existed for thousands of years. Empire-builders have long understood their importance. One example is the Lion of St Mark, complete with wings and a book, which was the symbol of imperial Venice. It stands on a column between St Mark's Square and the gondolas. Visitors to Bergamo, far away in the foothills of the Alps near Milan, are sometimes surprised to see the Lion of St Mark on the side of the Palazzo della Ragione. From the fifteenth to the eighteenth century the brand reminded people that they were in the Venetian Empire.

Corporate brands have existed for more than 400 years. The East India Company was founded in 1600. Since then corporate brands have sprung up in every developed economy. Examples include Benetton, Cadbury, Fosters, Guinness, L'Oréal, Mercedes, Nestlé, Nike, Samsung, Sony and Starbucks. In emerging markets, alcoholic drinks often lead the way and establish a global presence. Bars and clubs around the world sell Tiger Beer from Singapore and Brahma from Brazil, as well as Stolichnaya, the Russian vodka.

The word *brand* has been used in marketing since the mid-nineteenth century, when large factories began to produce soap and other packaged goods. People were used to buying such items from small producers in their local communities. However, the factory owners wanted their customers to trust a non-local product. When the product was ready for shipment, a red-hot iron was used to brand the factory's logo or insignia into the wooden container. Nowadays there are many definitions of a brand. One of our favourites is this: *a brand is a promise kept*. As Andy Milligan, a leading brand consultant, puts it: 'A brand is a symbol that guarantees a particular experience.'

By marketing a reliable, high-quality product, packaged goods manufacturers attracted millions of customers. Brands such as Kellogg's breakfast cereals gradually became as familiar as local farmers' produce. Manufacturers then learned to incorporate particular *brand values* – intangible characteristics that were important to consumers. Certain packaged foods were homely, for instance; they reminded you of the food your mother used to make. Later on they incorporated other brand values such as youthfulness, fun and luxury.

Developing a unique selling proposition

There are two main approaches to brand-building. The first is the *unique selling proposition* (USP), which is a powerful tool for attracting customers. Not every brand has a single feature that makes it unique. However, you can still have a USP based on a *unique combination* of benefits to the customer. For example, a cleaning fluid might remove both grease and limescale. A person could be good at both marketing and finance.

Some people aim to be the cheapest. However, there are several potential problems with this. First of all, if you only compete on price, you may earn very little. Secondly, any competitor can copy your USP at short notice – all they have to do is drop *their* price. The third problem is that being cheap will drive some customers away – they will interpret cheapness as a sign of poor quality. Top-quality products are sometimes described as 'reassuringly expensive'.

At this point it is worth clearing up two sources of confusion regarding the USP. Firstly, we are using the word *unique* in its literal sense. It is derived from the Latin word *unus*, meaning *one*. A product or service cannot be 'very unique': it is either unique or it is not. Secondly, confusion also arises when people talk about 'USPs' in the plural, listing advantages that competitors also offer, such as great customer service and a one-year guarantee. If several people have something, it is clearly not unique to anyone. Your USP can either be one characteristic or a unique combination of characteristics. A clear USP makes your brand stand out in people's minds.

The second approach to brand-building is *brand identity*. One of its strongest advocates was David Ogilvy, the founder of the Ogilvy advertising agency. He argued that brand identity was paramount. In his book *Confessions of an Advertising Man* he stated that advertisers should 'build sharply defined personalities for their brand and stick to those personalities year after year. It is the total personality of the brand rather than any trivial product difference which decides its position in the market place'.

Brand personalities develop over time, just like human personalities. Some have a heritage stretching back decades or centuries. Several generations from the same family know and love them. You can see this in luxury goods, banking, sports teams, private clubs, charities, cars, cameras, schools and universities. The key is to ensure that the brand identity remains consistent, while the products evolve and the brand itself grows. As we shall see in Chapter 7, *archetypes* are a valuable tool for managing this process.

Some of the most valuable brands have both a USP and a strong brand identity. For example, Coca-Cola has a unique recipe and a brand identity that is known worldwide.

Evolving to meet changing needs

As society evolves, brands must keep up. Attitudes to nutrition and the environment have changed fast, catching some companies off-guard. In the media sector, the switch from print to digital has left some businesses behind. During a period of change, the winners remain true to their *values*: deeply held beliefs that they communicate continuously. Their values enable them to retain existing customers and attract new ones.

In some cases they develop a vocabulary to express what they stand for. Tesco has been very successful at this. Britain's largest food retailer operates in Europe and Asia. It also owns Fresh & Easy in the USA. Since 1994 its tag line has been *every little helps.*

Instead of making extravagant claims which critics can ridicule, it focuses on small, continuous improvements. This slogan has proved highly adaptable. For a long period *every little helps* meant helping the customer save money through low prices. Then more and more people became concerned about wasteful packaging and the need to recycle. Tesco responded by using the same slogan in a new series of advertisements. These showed ordinary people and celebrities transporting their shopping without using plastic bags. A bricklayer carried his groceries on a hod which is normally used for bricks. John McEnroe took a green apple from a tube of tennis balls and began chomping away on it. The phrase *every little helps* has worked consistently during a period of rapid change.

Chapter

3

Personal branding:
the essentials

As we said earlier, your brand is what people say about you when you are not in the room. What if someone you know described you to someone you had never met? What would they say? They might talk about the kind of work you do. For example: 'She's a troubleshooter. She turns things around.' They might say where you used to work or where you were educated. They might mention your physical appearance, or a sport or hobby that is important to you. If you are related to someone famous, they would probably mention that, too.

We will show you how to turn your brand into a valuable asset – perhaps your most valuable asset. As with any other brand, your personal brand is based on people's expectations of how you will behave or perform in particular circumstances. The stronger your track record, the more confidence they will have in you. Your brand is a promise kept. It can be communicated through symbols such as your name, your physical appearance or the way you speak and write. Some people even have their own typeface or logo.

Your brand consists of both reputation and reach

You may have a good *reputation*, but that is not the same thing as your brand. The Latin root of the word reputation is *reputare* – to think repeatedly. There may be five people who think about you often and ask you to work with them now and then. However, what if 50 or 500 people kept thinking about you? How much busier and wealthier would you be? The greater the number of people who think about you, the greater is your *reach*. The two dimensions of your brand are shown in the diagram.

The more often someone thinks of you, and the higher their opinion of you, the stronger your reputation becomes. The larger the number of people who think about you, the greater your reach becomes. In order to build a strong brand, you need both reach and reputation.

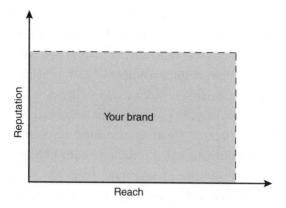

Your brand needs to be actively managed

Your brand is not static, it is constantly developing. If you are employed, your brand affects your visibility and your job prospects. It also determines the number and quality of job offers you receive from other employers. If you are running a business, your brand will help you win customers and raise money on favourable terms. If you are an investor, your brand will help you attract high-quality opportunities from management teams, advisers and other investors.

Most people have weak brands. When you come back from a conference with a handful of business cards, it is hard to remember who was who, let alone what they did or how you might be able to work with them. As Jonathan Guthrie of the *Financial Times* once said: 'Did he import china from Turkey, or turkeys from China?'

If you want to be successful, you must stand out from the crowd. People should remember who you are, what you do and what makes you different. The stronger your brand, the more people will value you. They will be pleased that *you* are working on their project and may pay extra for that feeling of reassurance. Anyone can build a strong brand, including electricians, disc jockeys, plumbers, cleaners, psychotherapists, lecturers and portrait painters.

The professional services sector, including consultants, lawyers and accountants, has grown rapidly. Some professionals spend many years with the same firm, but the issue of personal branding still arises. If you are a junior member of staff, it helps to be well regarded by several partners, since they will decide who works on each project. They may also support your election to the partnership. Once you become a partner, you suddenly find yourself in a sales role, required to win a certain amount of business. Your personal brand is now more important than ever. Some partners rely heavily on their firm's brand, which can help to ensure they are invited to pitch for new projects. However, it is better to build your personal brand too, so clients ask specifically for you, wherever you happen to be working.

Your brand should be authentic and consistent

A powerful brand has to be *authentic*: based on who you are and what your life and work are all about. You should aim to be the best *you*. Some people project an image that does not fit reality, often by imitating a person they admire or by attempting to conform. The result is artificial and unconvincing. They are sometimes described as *cardboard cut-outs*.

As we said in Chapter 1, the key to building your brand is to know yourself. The first step is to identify the *talents* you were born with. It is best to develop them in a distinctive way, in accordance with your *values*. If you are authentic, people will know what you do and what you stand for. Some people will keep away from you, others will be attracted to you. If you make it easy for people to see what you do and how you do it, their perception will be aligned with reality. If you then extend your brand into a new area, it will make sense to them; they will feel comfortable working with you in a different situation.

You may wish to keep your work and private lives separate. However, it is still a good idea to be consistent. You do not have to tell everyone about your private life, but it helps if what you say in private does not clash with what you say at work or in public. This is particularly important on social networking sites. There are countless examples of people losing their jobs after criticising their employers online. It is best to assume that everything you write on a social networking site is public. At the very least, someone can copy what you have written and paste it anywhere they like.

The more authentic you are, the more attractive you will be to some people and the less attractive you will be to others. (If you try to please everyone you will fail to appeal strongly to anyone.) Those who are attracted to you will feel they can rely on you to behave in a certain way.

Self-employed people often have a natural overlap between their work and their social lives. Friends may become customers or colleagues, and vice versa. If so, it is essential to be the same person at work and elsewhere. Your life will then be integrated and harmonious. Instead of wearing different masks, you can be yourself in every situation.

Your brand can become valuable

A strong brand will make you stand out in the eyes of people who want what you have to offer. They will naturally think of you. If your brand appeals to them, they will choose you. They may even pay a premium to work with you. However, if you do not stand out, they will see you as a *commodity*. Having no particular reason to choose you, they will pay you the going rate at best. Top musicians and film stars illustrate this principle. Their fans buy their latest album or watch their latest film because they are in it. They earn far more than other musicians or actors. The extra money they earn is only partly due to their singing or acting ability. Film, television and digital media have given them a global market that has boosted their earnings enormously.

Personal brands can also acquire an influence that goes way beyond money. Mahatma Gandhi, Nelson Mandela and Mother Teresa have all shaped our world by embodying and promoting a set of *values*, as have Che Guevara, Bob Marley and Mao Zedong.

Some people behave as though they do not have a brand, or if they do, it is worth nothing to them. Some entrepreneurs treat their investors badly when they raise money for a business, assuming they will do so only once. This can make it difficult, if not impossible, to raise money for a second venture. Other entrepreneurs focus on serving their customers *and* their investors. They develop a following which helps to make their second business even more successful than the first.

Some interview candidates over-promise and under-deliver. They look good on paper. They sound good when you meet them. However, when you investigate their track record, you find they have achieved little for their employers. They often lack authenticity, claiming to have certain values but behaving in an entirely different way. This damages their brand and their job prospects.

Your brand can outlive you

A personal brand can last for decades, even centuries, continuing to sell products and services. Think of Mozart, Elvis Presley, Nina Simone, Albert Camus, Charles Dickens, Jane Austen and Lao Tsu, author of the *Tao Te Ching* over 2,500 years ago. William Shakespeare's brand still generates revenues for the Royal Shakespeare Company, the Globe Theatre in London and his home town of Stratford-upon-Avon.

You do not have to be a celebrity for your brand to outlive you and reach new people. John's father, Ken, was a photographer whose work was published in books and magazines about the countryside. His photos now appeal to a wider market than ever, including a new generation of city-dwellers.

Your name is part of your brand

Your name should be memorable and encourage word-of-mouth advertising. More and more of us work in a global market. Can people from other countries remember your name and pronounce it? In some cases a stage name may be the answer. Hence Gordon Sumner became Sting and Paul Hewson became Bono. Madonna Ciccone is known simply as Madonna. Alliteration can also work well, as it has for the artists Gilbert & George.

You may be blessed with an unusual name, but if it is difficult to pronounce, it can hinder word-of-mouth advertising. One solution is to adapt it, as Vincent Van Gogh did when he left the Netherlands to work in Belgium and France. Since he knew his surname would be difficult for foreigners to pronounce, he signed his paintings simply as *Vincent*.

Another approach is to explain the pronunciation in a memorable way. Elisabeth Tschyrkow is an American whose parents were born in Russia. People pronounce her surname in various ways. Some do not even try. The danger is they will remember her as 'the American lady with the unpronounceable name'. Her solution is to write the following on her CV and elsewhere:

Elisabeth Tschyrkow
(pronounced 'Cheer-Co')

Maximilian Thurlow is a young journalist whose full name appears on most documents, including his CV. However, 'Maximilian' is rather long, with lots of syllables. Most people call him Max. From a branding point of view, *Max Thurlow* works much better. It is easier to pronounce and remember.

If you have a common name, such as John Smith, you can differentiate yourself by using a middle initial – or creating one.

If you change your surname, it is harder for people to find out what you have done. That may be helpful if you have a criminal record. Otherwise you may wish to keep your achievements visible. If you are getting married and are well known in your market, you will need to make a decision about your surname. One option is to add your spouse's surname to the end of your own. For example, if Susan Bailey marries Fred Walker, she may choose to change her name to Susan Bailey Walker both socially and at work. As far as the internet is concerned, it is better not to place a hyphen between Bailey and Walker. That way, search engines will still pick up 'Susan Bailey', whether she appears in a professional or a social capacity. You can also set up a personal website that people will find easily if they search for your new or old names on the Web. We will discuss this in Chapter 17.

Another option is to change your surname but leave a trail online, so that people can still find you under your old surname. For example, if Susan decides to change her name from Susan Bailey to Susan Walker, she can keep her personal website and any pages on Facebook, LinkedIn, Twitter, Google+ etc. that describe her as Susan Bailey. On each website she can tell visitors that her name has changed to Susan Walker and provide links to the new locations where she appears under her new name. That way, her old contacts will still be able to find her.

Your appearance is part of your brand

If you have ever interviewed students for graduate traineeships, you will understand the advantage of having a memorable appearance. At the end of a full day of interviews, you have met several people in their early twenties. Most of the men have short hair, wear dark suits and are studying similar subjects. It is very difficult to distinguish one from the other. The women have the advantage of variety. You might remember the one with the bright red outfit or the long black hair.

Your appearance is a key part of your brand identity, so it is worth devoting time and effort to it. Some people are so distinctive that they are instantly recognisable. Here are some examples:

- Albert Einstein's moustache and wild hairstyle.
- Che Guevara's beard and beret.
- Margaret Thatcher's hairdo, blue outfit and handbag.
- Winston Churchill's bald head, waistcoat and cigar.
- Mick Jagger's tongue and lips, which became the logo of the Rolling Stones.
- Groucho Marx's handlebar moustache, thick eyebrows and round glasses.
- Marilyn Monroe's blonde hair, dark eyebrows and pouting lips.

We will discuss appearance in more detail in Chapter 12.

Your job title is not your brand

Some people aspire to a certain title, such as partner, director or chief executive, and cling to it once they have it. They assume that this is who they are. However, your title tells people little or nothing about what you do or what you stand for. It does not make you unique. At most it indicates your position in a hierarchy, and perhaps the skills you possess.

A former colleague of ours has turned around ten companies, including some large, well-known ones. Although his current title is chief executive, he views it purely as a tool to do his job. Sometimes it is an inconvenience. He describes himself as a *turnaround guy*, which is far more meaningful.

Your brand should stand out like a tall building

Imagine your brand is a building under construction – you want it to be distinctive and clearly visible. Think of the Eiffel Tower, the Empire State Building or the Taj Mahal. As it becomes bigger and taller, more and more people will notice it. They will start to ask what goes on inside.

However, before you build it, you must first prepare the ground. This brings us to the subject of your talents.

Chapter

Your talents

The dictionary provides two definitions of the word *talent*. The first is a natural ability to do something well. The second is a person of exceptional ability. However, the word talent is sometimes used to describe 'anyone we employ and therefore have to manage'. There are even 'talent pools', apparently. We prefer to stick to the dictionary. Your brand should be based on your talents – the things you naturally do well.

If your brand is a building, your talents are the bedrock on which it is built. Talents emerge at any time from early childhood onwards. Education can help you discover them. The words *educate* and *education* are derived from a Latin verb meaning *to draw out*. The educator draws out something that is already within you. With training and experience, a talent can be developed into one or more *skills*. Ironically, since our talents come naturally to us, it is easy to neglect them. Some people even focus on their weaknesses instead.

Your talents manifest themselves in what you enjoy most and do best. If you think back to when you really enjoyed your work – and did a great job – you will probably find you were using your talents effectively. You were able to do what was needed and everything fell into place. It may have seemed effortless. People often become immersed and lose track of time.

Psychologist Mihaly Csikszentmihalyi describes these optimal experiences as *flow*. You are likely to experience *flow* when you combine your talents in ways you find meaningful, pursuing goals that are attainable while feeling in control of the process and receiving positive feedback. *Flow experiences* help you identify your talents. They also show you the ways of using your talents that you find most fulfilling.

Identifying your talents

The best way to identify your talents is to examine what you have done in the past. Ask people who know you well to help you. They will remember you in different situations.

Please note that talents are not the same as skills. Talents are innate. You are born with them and cannot change them. For this reason they are sometimes described as *gifts*. Over time you can develop skills that are based on your talents. Examples of talents include:

■ Using humour to lighten the mood of a group.

■ Easily spotting a mistake in a page of words or numbers.

■ Capturing the essence of an argument in a few simple words.

■ Capturing the hearts and minds of a group of people engaged in a task.

This brings us to our first exercise.

Exercise A: Your talents

(a) Reflect on your life and identify at least seven occasions that you recall as *high points* or *peak experiences*. (It doesn't matter how old you were when these high points occurred.) These are memories of times that gave you a great sense of pleasure or achievement. They are highly *meaningful* for you. List them in the spaces below. Take them from different areas of your life, including your childhood, education, work and leisure pursuits.

1 ....

2 ....

3 ....

4 ....

5 ....

6 ....

7 ....

If you recall more than seven high points, write the extra ones down, too. The more high points you have on the sheet of paper in front of you, the easier it will be to identify themes emerging from them.

Be careful not to select events just because you consider them socially acceptable or likely to impress others. Choose those that are meaningful for *you*.

(b) For each high point, ask yourself:

▪ Which talents was I using and enjoyed using the most?

▪ With what kind of people?

▪ In what type of situation?

(c) Now list your talents, starting with those that give you the most energy when you use them.

1 ....

2 ....

3 ....

4 ....

5 ....

6 ....

7 .... etc.

Are there any common themes connecting your high points? If so, write them down.

This is an open-ended exercise. As you go through the other exercises, further high points will emerge. Sometimes those you had forgotten turn out to be particularly significant. It is important to ask people who have known you at different stages of your life for their views. They may remember experiences that you had forgotten.

If *none* of your high points has occurred in your chosen profession or business, it is worth asking yourself whether you are working in the right area. High points can provide clues about other ways of applying your talents more enjoyably and profitably. Equally, if all your high points are in the distant past, it is worth asking yourself whether the path you have taken recently is right for you. Maybe there is another that would suit you better.

Once you've completed the exercise, take a moment to reflect. How do you feel about where you have come from and where you are going? What are the underlying themes? We will discuss these in later chapters.

We strongly encourage you to complete this exercise, which has helped people in many occupations.

Below are two examples, Henry and Elizabeth. Henry is in his early forties. He is British and works in a bank in Geneva. Elizabeth is in her early thirties. She grew up in Hong Kong and works in the UK in sales and marketing.

Henry and Elizabeth

This is what Henry discovered about himself:

(a) Reflect on your life and identify seven occasions that you recall as *high points* or *peak experiences*.

1 Working on a local farm from the age of seven. This was where I discovered my love of horse riding.

2 Playing football and becoming captain of the school team, while doing fairly badly in my studies.

3 Having scraped into university to study history, suddenly beginning to enjoy my work and graduating in the top quartile.

4 Taking a year off to work as a volunteer on a project in East Africa.

5 Getting my first job in banking.

6 The successful project that put me on the fast track for promotion.

7 Developing a computer program that transformed how people worked.

(b) and (c) Based on his seven high points, Henry identified some key themes running through the talents that he both enjoyed and used the most. They are shown below. He realised that he naturally used his talents in situations where he felt he could make a difference. He particularly enjoyed working with intellectual people, in situations where his understanding of people and his talent for persuasion were valued.

Here are his talents ranked in descending order of importance to him:

1 Examining a complex situation and identifying the simplest solution.

2 Listening carefully and persuading people to take the appropriate action.

3 Identifying people's strengths and weaknesses.

4 Building confidence within teams.

5 Identifying patterns of behaviour that cause problems.

6 Taking measured risks that raise my level of confidence.

These six talents are based on Henry's peak experiences from the age of seven. Like many of us, Henry has certain talents that he *cannot stop* using. He has a deeply ingrained habit of solving other people's problems. When he looked back over the high points in his life, the theme of solving problems was always there. He loves analysing complex situations and then devising practical solutions.

Here are Elizabeth's high points:

1   Getting the lead role in the school play at the age of seven.

2   Organising a charity fundraising event at school that raised twice as much money as it had the year before.

3   Being elected president of the students' union at university.

4   Winning a place on my new employer's graduate training scheme.

5   A one-year assignment in France, where I learned to speak French.

6   Becoming my company's youngest-ever female brand manager.

7   Playing a key role in winning an industry gold award for the best public relations campaign.

Based on this exercise, Elizabeth concluded that she had constantly used her ability to learn quickly to help her achieve results. She also realised that she always needed a situation that was both complex and exciting in order to get motivated.

Elizabeth thought about her talents and the themes she felt she could not ignore. She then drew up a list of her talents, ranked in descending order of importance to her:

1   Strong powers of persuasion.

2   Selling ideas and products.

3   Spotting trends and capitalising on them.

4   Analysing numbers, including financial statements.

5   Adapting quickly to new cultures and ways of working.

Elizabeth has a knack of persuading people to do things and getting them done profitably. Her confidence and persuasiveness, combined with a facility for numbers, have helped her succeed in her career to date.

We encourage you to do this first exercise thoroughly. It is the basis of everything that follows. One of the many benefits is that you will have a collection of stories you can tell other people to explain how you use your talents (even if you do not use the word *talents* when talking to them). Stories are particularly useful in an interview. As the saying goes: 'Facts tell. Stories sell.'

Most of the time, you may illustrate your talents by talking about high points that have occurred during your work. However, some people also tell stories from their childhood that illustrate a particular talent. For example, an entrepreneur might talk about a business they set up at school. A musician might describe their first performance at the age of five.

Some people have one talent which makes them stand out. However, for most of us it is a *combination* of talents that makes us unique.

Exercise B: Your combination of talents

Look at the list of talents you wrote down at the end of Exercise A. How have you combined them in ways that you really enjoyed? How could you do so in the future?

One example is the way Henry often combined his talent for identifying people's strengths and weaknesses with his talent for building confidence within teams.

Elizabeth realised that she often combined her talent for selling ideas and products with her talent for spotting trends and capitalising on them.

Once you have completed the talents exercises it is time to look at your *values*.

Chapter

5

Your values

As we said in the previous chapter, if your brand is a building, then your talents are the bedrock on which it rests. Your values are the foundations. Although your values are below the surface, they determine the shape of the building. If you apply your talents in accordance with your values, you can build a very strong brand.

Identifying your values

Your values are *what you believe is important*. They are evident in the *way* you do things. Values can range from a belief in hard work or punctuality to deeper principles such as self-reliance, concern for others or harmony with the environment.

Two people with identical talents but dissimilar values are likely to pursue entirely different careers. Imagine two equally talented pianists. One is introspective, deeply religious and shuns the limelight. He becomes an organist in a cathedral. The other is an extrovert, loves travel and is excited by the idea of performing in front of large audiences. She becomes a concert pianist. Knowing your values can also help you decide how to apply your talents and build a fulfilling career. You will know which types of work are right for you and which are not. Being true to your values makes you authentic and helps you stand out from the crowd. You become like a magnet, attracting people who hold similar values, whether they are customers, colleagues or suppliers.

The first step is to *identify* your values. The second step is to *project* them. The following exercise will help you.

Exercise C: What you admire in others

Write down the names of all the people you admire most, in the space below. Include friends and neighbours, close or distant members of your family, world leaders, authors, artists, sportspeople, media personalities, colleagues and so on. Include the living and the dead. You can also include fictional characters, from television, film or literature. Write down as many as possible – aim for at least 20.

Name

1 ....
2 ....
3 ....
4 ....
5 ....
6 ....
7 ....
8 ....
9 ....
10 ....
11 ....
12 ....
13 ....
14 ....
15 ....
16 ....
17 ....
18 ....
19 ....
20 ....
21 ....
22 ....

23 ....

24 ....

25 ....

Now for the second step. Take another look at your list above. Next
to each name, write down all the qualities for which you admire
this person. Here are some possibilities. We are not suggesting you
should admire them for any of these attributes, they are just examples:
confidence, beauty, persuasiveness, putting their family first, physical
fitness, good company, enthusiasm, articulacy, intelligence, honesty,
serenity, sincerity, healthy lifestyle, kindness, fighting for what they
believe in, hard-working, insightful, loyal to a particular cause, supportive,
witty, clarity of thought, sound judgement.

We are interested in each person's character or behaviour. If you see the
same quality in a number of the people you admire, you should write it
down for each of them.

The third step is to review what you have written and think about
the qualities you admire in others. Themes will emerge. You will see a
number of qualities repeated in slightly different ways. Which of these
qualities *resonate* most for you? Consider those that appeal to you
rationally, emotionally and spiritually. These *qualities* reflect your *values*
(the qualities you admire in other people).

In the space below, write down the five values that matter most to you,
starting with the most important:

1 ....

2 ....

3 ....

4 ....

5 ....

Adapted from Life\Work Design, Crystal Barkley Corporation

Henry and Elizabeth

When Henry completed this exercise he produced the following list of people, with the reasons why he admired them:

1 Muhammad Ali – brilliant at what he did. Used his celebrity status for a cause.

2 Carl Lewis – a great athlete.

3 Bob Geldof – passionate about changing the world.

4 Captain Scott – a courageous adventurer who risked everything.

5 Ellen MacArthur – determined to succeed.

6 My father – amiable, good with people, pragmatic and charming.

7 My mother – witty, intelligent, hard-working, resourceful, with strong morals.

8 Tim (a friend of mine) – intelligent, kind, thoughtful, great at managing teams.

9 Sebastian (another friend) – stoical, thoughtful, energetic, fights for what he believes in.

10 Nelson Mandela – courageous. Fought for his beliefs. Suffered but forgave his captors.

11 Martin Luther King – a courageous campaigner who died for a cause.

12 Steve Redgrave – committed, with the grit to carry on.

13 Alex Ferguson – a wonderful appetite for success over a long period.

14 Tony Benn – a politician and statesman without ego.

15 Peter Cook – a wonderfully innovative comedian.

16 Kelly Holmes – overcame injury and persevered to reach her goal.

17 Neil Armstrong – a courageous adventurer who risked everything.

18 Aung San Suu Kyi – a courageous campaigner who risked everything for her cause.

19 Terry Waite – imprisoned while promoting peace and understanding.

20 Stuart Rose – visionary, tough, a good manager.

21 Richard (my ex-boss) – quiet, gets on with it, brilliant mind, confident.

22 George (our former CEO) – engaging, clever, hard-working, strong values.

23 Gerald (ex-colleague) – intelligent, strong self-belief, entrepreneurial.

24 Helen (ex-boss) – genius, financial wizard, multi-talented, charming.

25 Margaret Thatcher – visionary, intelligent, stubborn, insatiable appetite for work.

Based on this list, Henry identified the following values, in order of importance to him:

1 Courage.

2 Hard work.

3 Risk taking.

4 Loyalty.

5 Modesty.

6 Service to others.

He realised that he had been expressing his values through the following activities:

▓ working hard to find solutions to complex problems;

▓ developing new ways of working that are more practical and effective;

▓ developing his team's strengths through challenging projects.

Here is Elizabeth's list of people she admires:

1 Richard Branson – has made money and enjoys himself.

2 Bill Gates – has made money. Set up a foundation that supports millions of people.

3 Jill (a friend) – worked her way up from the bottom to become a successful business person.

4 John (ex-boss) – intelligent, thoughtful, not motivated by personal wealth.

5 My grandmother – worked hard all her life but was always happy and helpful.

6 Parents – overcame health problems without complaint and got on with life.

7 Frank Lloyd Wright – inspirational architect.

8 Le Corbusier – used his talents to devise a new way of living.

9 Antonio Gaudí – inspired loyalty to his individualistic point of view.

10 Norman Foster – imaginative designs that inspire.

11 Frank Gehry – modern art/architecture at its best.

12 Francisco Goya – amazing painter. Not afraid to paint what he saw.

13 Albrecht Dürer – incredible attention to detail.

14 Lucian Freud – shocking, provocative art.

15 Kit McMahon – intelligent banker who broke the mould.

16 Henry (ex-finance director) – took the time to explain financial modelling to me.

17 My maths teacher – for his patience and understanding.

18 My drama teacher – for giving me confidence.

19 David Ogilvy – for giving personality to brands.

20 Tim (ex-boss) – for having the confidence to let me loose!

21 Jean (friend) – for always being there, always supportive.

22 Bob (my husband) – for being a rock. When I am rushing around sorting everyone else out, he looks after me.

23 Amy and Scilla (daughters) – for the joy they bring to my life.

From this list Elizabeth identified her top five values:

1 Determination.

2 Being positive in the face of difficulty.

3 Inspirational leadership.

4 Intelligence.

5 Innovation.

Please note that when we talk about your values, we are talking about the *way* you use your talents. You will almost certainly have a different set of talents than the people you admire. For example, *determination* is a quality that Elizabeth admires in other people. It is therefore one of her values. Her talents are different from theirs. However, she and they apply their talents with determination. For her, determination has to do with:

■ not being afraid to be different;

■ being clear about what she wants to achieve;

■ knowing that she is supported by those around her;

■ using her communication skills to create support for her actions;

■ recognising the difficulties that could emerge from her actions.

Elizabeth values determination in herself and others. She understands the way she exhibits determination in using her talents to build a business.

Both Henry and Elizabeth found it helpful to understand their values. They also mentioned situations where their values had not been respected. This had made them feel uncomfortable, so they had moved on at the earliest opportunity.

Think about organisations where you have worked, and your colleagues at that time. Can you see now why they were right or wrong for you? Think about the work you are doing now. You may feel there is a mismatch between your work and your values. However, maybe the *work* is right for you but the *situation* is wrong. Some people do well for years in a particular role. Then they move to another organisation where they do badly. Is it them or is it the situation? It frequently turns out that the work is aligned with their talents, just as before. However, there is a clash between their values and the values of the organisation they have joined. If you discover that your values clash with the work itself, it is worth considering any changes you could make. The strongest brands are built by people doing what they love, in a situation that is compatible with their values.

Knowing your values is a great help in building and leading teams. A client of ours is a chief executive who keeps a large white board in his office, with his values written on it. Everyone can see them when they go there for meetings. His values have helped him change the organisation's culture and lead over a thousand people in a new direction. Anyone he interviews can see what he values in other people. They can then decide whether they want to work with him.

If you want to look more deeply into your values, you can also consider the *things* you admire. Write down all the things in your life that have had some meaning for you. They can range from your favourite teddy bear to an interest in architecture to the latest camera or an amazing sunset. The qualities you admire in these things will give your values another dimension.

Fulfilling your potential

In many cases, the qualities we admire in others are those we have yet to acknowledge in ourselves. We may even have suppressed them for some reason. In the meantime we 'project' these qualities onto other people.

Once you acknowledge this you can reclaim each quality and make it your own. If you admire people who are highly creative, it may be time for you to be more creative. If you admire people who are influential, it may be time for you to exert more influence. You do not have to give up your current job or business. You can start right now, exactly where you are.

The following exercise will help you examine this more closely.

Exercise D: Who could you become?

Look back at what you wrote for Exercise C on page 39. Look at the people you admire. In some or all cases you may feel that you do not have their particular talent or combination of talents. Now look at the *way* they use their talents. Could you use your talents in the same way – or a similar way – to the way they use their talents?

For example, John admires several singer-songwriters. In his teens he tried playing the guitar and singing, together with a friend, Roger Wilson, who later became a professional folk singer. John discovered that he did not have Roger's musical talent. However, he admires certain singer-songwriters' *creativity* in writing new material and their *confidence* in reaching a large, international audience. In the meantime he has discovered that he does have a talent for writing and public speaking. He therefore uses his talents in accordance with his values, by writing and speaking for a large, international audience.

Chapter

Your purpose

So far, we have talked about your talents and your values. Your talents are the bedrock on which your brand is built. You can discover them but you cannot change them. Your values are the foundations. Although they are below the surface, they determine the size and shape of the building. Buildings also have a *purpose*. A building can be an office, a fire station, a house, a hospital, a theatre or a laboratory, for example.

Our next topic is your purpose: why you are on the planet. This is a fundamental issue. Small children have been known to point to an adult and ask, 'What is he for?'

The idea that each of us has a purpose is new to many people and is often confused with goals or objectives. This diagram will help to clarify the subject.

Adapted from Life\Work Design, Crystal Barkley Corporation

Goals/objectives, plans and tasks are *finite*. Sooner or later you can complete a task, carry out a plan or achieve a goal. Then you can remove it from your to-do list. Your purpose and your mission, however, are *infinite*.

Your purpose ranks above all else. It is the direction that is right for you. Your purpose arises from your talents and your values. It is like the horizon: you will never get there. You can pursue your purpose for the rest of your life. Therapist and life coach Martha Beck calls it your *North Star*.

The fact that your purpose is infinite makes it hard – if not impossible – to pin down. It may become clear only towards the end of your life. Albert Einstein once said: 'Strange is our situation here upon the earth. Each of us comes here for a short visit, not knowing why, yet sometimes seeming to divine a purpose.' Fortunately it is enough to have a *sense of purpose*, i.e. a sense of direction. You do not necessarily have to put it into words; you just have a feeling about whether you are heading in the right direction for you.

You know you are pursuing your purpose when your whole being seems to resonate with what you are doing. You may feel a rush of energy and enthusiasm when you are *active* in a particular situation, however fleeting it may be.

Discovering your mission

Below your purpose is your *mission*, which describes how you want to live your life and what you want to do. In this chapter we will show you how to draft your *mission statement*. It will be expansive rather than limiting, recognising the fact that you will often find yourself at a crossroads. Your mission statement will help to guide you towards the path that will be most fulfilling, both now and in the future.

If you do not understand your mission, you may feel like a hamster on a wheel, going round and round from one goal to the next without any meaning in your life.

Your mission is infinite, just like your purpose. However, most people find it much easier to define their mission. It will give you a stronger sense of purpose. It will also help other people to decide whether they want to work with you. It is an essential tool for building your brand.

Discovering what you can't stop doing

You can gain valuable insights into your mission and purpose by looking at the things you cannot stop doing. When you are immersed in these activities, you are likely to lose track of time. This experience has been given many names. Athletes often call it 'being in the zone'. You do not think about what you are doing, you just do it. For example, Henry often loses track of time when he is looking for simple solutions to complex problems. On one occasion, someone told him a problem could not be solved so he started working on it when he got home. When he finally stopped for a cup of coffee he realised it was 4am!

Similarly, the 'turnaround guy' we mentioned in Chapter 3 cannot resist reviving a business in distress. This is based on his under-lying values, which include hard work, never giving up and acting with a strong social conscience. The talents he applies include analysis, planning, negotiating and persuading people to take action. Every organisation he deals with has a unique set of prob-lems, so he is always developing and improving his skills.

In many cases your friends will be aware of the things you cannot stop doing – maybe more so than you are. John asked some friends for their feedback on this. He also thought about his high points from the Talents exercise on pages 31–2. Then he produced the following list of things he cannot stop doing:

- Introducing people who might be able to help each other.
- Putting together teams of people to help transform companies.
- Helping people to develop a new business, book or film.
- Reading and giving talks about psychology, Eastern philosophy and personal development.
- Writing books, blog posts and articles that will help people to fulfil their potential.
- Connecting with people on Facebook and Twitter.
- Taking photographs, particularly of people he knows and of scenes he encounters while travelling.

Here are some things that David cannot stop doing:

- Helping organisations to develop processes that encourage staff to use more of their potential.

- Creating harmony through the juxtaposition of elements, such as (a) furniture in a room or (b) exciting new ways in which someone can develop their talents.

- Encouraging individuals to fulfil the potential that David sees in them.

- Writing and speaking on subjects related to career management.

- Training teams of people to understand each other's contributions and use them for everyone's benefit.

- Designing gardens that can grow more beautiful year by year.

- Provoking people in a friendly way, to help them wake up to reality.

Now it is your turn.

Exercise E: What can't you stop doing?

Think back to the Talents exercise on page 31. Your high points may reveal an activity that you are often pursuing when you experience a high point. If you ask other people how they perceive you, they may say you have a passion for something that is more obvious to them than it is to you. Ask your friends and/or family to tell you about the things you cannot stop doing. Make a list of all the things you keep doing, whether or not anyone pays you to do them. Include any activity, whether you have labelled it as work, fun, a hobby, a distraction, or anything else.

....

....

....

....

....

....

....

Once you have your list of things you cannot stop doing, you can begin to identify the themes that connect them. For example, in John's case:

- He can see that *connecting people* is something he does naturally. Every now and then, the people he has introduced do something amazing together.

- When he meets people who have an idea, he automatically thinks about how it could be developed further.

- Much of his writing is about transforming people's careers and their lives, and helping the world to change.

- He sees photography as transforming an everyday scene into something meaningful. It also celebrates people's individuality.

In David's case there are also some clear themes:

- Being a catalyst for developing individuals, groups and even gardens, by helping to uncover more of their potential.

- Getting a buzz out of the 'ah ha' moment when people catch sight of their potential and are energised by it.

- Reaching out to people through training events and conferences, and writing books that encourage them to manage their careers.

- Working with organisations to help them change the way they manage and develop their people.

These themes are so strong that if David gets into a discussion with someone about their career, he can easily lose track of time and miss his next appointment.

Now it is your turn again.

Exercise F: Which themes underlie the things you can't stop doing?

Jot down any idea that comes to mind:

....

....

....

....

....

....

....

Once you have identified the themes, you can start to think about your mission. A good way to do this is to work on your mission statement. It forces you to be clear and concise. For example, John has distilled what he does into the following mission statement:

I help people to transform their businesses, their careers and their lives.

His mission is unlimited, in the sense that he will never run out of people to help. However, this statement makes the direction he is taking clear to him and to everyone else.

For David, the following statement encapsulates what he does:

Helping individuals and organisations to identify their talents, values and purpose, so they can lead truly satisfying lives.

The more David works with people, the more he learns about different ways to support them in their quest – and the more he realises he needs to learn.

Now it is your turn.

Exercise G: Your mission statement

Use a large, blank sheet of paper or a flipchart so you can write down the key insights as soon as they occur to you. Now look back over the exercises you have completed so far.

1 When you look at what you have written, what are the themes that emerge? What is it that you cannot stop doing? What gives you boundless energy?

2 Describe how you work, in a paragraph.

3 Now distil this paragraph into a phrase or sentence that you can use as a mission statement, in draft form.

4 Test this mission statement on people who know you well. Work with it. Refine it as you go.

It is worth taking the time to define your mission, rather than simply leaping at opportunities. Once you understand your mission, it will be much easier to identify opportunities that resonate for you.

Pursuing your mission

Once you are clear about your mission, your work will be much more meaningful and satisfying. You will have a strong sense of purpose. This will enable you to build a powerful brand and be much more successful. Then you can choose goals that fit your mission. Understanding your mission will also enable you to eliminate goals that do not fit.

Unfortunately, a lot of people skip the first step. They are unaware of their mission, so they spend their lives pursuing goals. They are constantly striving towards the next qualification, or job, or material possession, or retirement. They may never attain some of these goals. Even if they do, what comes next?

The usual reaction is to set another goal, and another, and another. You may be busy planning and taking action, but the satisfaction from achieving goals in isolation is short-lived. It is like being a hamster on a wheel: running hard to achieve a sales target, to save a sum of money or to lose a certain amount of weight. Setting and achieving arbitrary goals does not answer the question: *Why?* Why are you doing what you do? If you do not know, you may wake up one day and realise that your life is meaningless. Pursuing endless goals can lead to problems. For example, there are many sportspeople who become unhappy once their physical abilities decline. Many successful business people die shortly after retirement. We will come back to the subject of goals below.

Pursuing your mission could mean that you follow a recognised career path. Equally, you might do things that make more sense to you than they do to other people – at least for the time being. George Orwell, the author and essayist, experienced many facets of life that enriched his writing. Following his education at Eton College, he worked in Burma, lived among the homeless, worked at the BBC in London and fought in the Spanish Civil War. These influences are evident in his writing, including *Down and Out in Paris and London, Animal Farm* and *Nineteen Eighty-Four.*

Paul Whitehouse, the comedy scriptwriter and actor, has done a wide range of jobs, including stacking shelves in supermarkets. As a result he writes and performs material that everyone can relate to, regardless of their background. He draws sharp contrasts between different social groups and the ways they behave.

Some successful career moves are the result of an accident or illness. One example is Jonathan Shaw, whose young son developed eczema followed by a nut and egg allergy. Realising that other parents of allergic children needed help to find the right products and services, Jonathan launched The Allergy & Free From Show, an exhibition that now takes place annually.

Jobs, businesses, books, etc. are *vehicles* for pursuing your mission. For example, Deepak Chopra is an endocrinologist who no longer treats patients individually. He has written dozens of books on mind/body medicine and spiritual topics, and speaks to audiences all over the world. Another example is Albert Schweitzer, who was, among other things, a doctor and a gifted musician. He used the proceeds from his recitals of Bach's organ works to finance a hospital in French Equatorial Africa. He wrote several books and was awarded the Nobel Peace Prize.

Top athletes train hard for years in pursuit of their goals, such as being the best at what they do. Once they retire, it is important for them to pursue their mission/purpose in other ways, one of which might be to act as a role model for young athletes and support them in fulfilling their potential. In the UK, David Lloyd is now better known for his health clubs than his ability as a tennis player.

People with a clear sense of purpose often find several ways to express it. Many of them never retire. They continue to pursue their mission, moving from one way of expressing it to another. Doing what they love gives them energy. They may even say they are putting their heart and soul into their work. Some people carry on working long after they have enough money to last a lifetime. Pablo Picasso once said that when he worked, he relaxed. Doing nothing made him tired.

Once you identify and pursue your mission, it pervades your life. Other people see it in you, in a variety of contexts. You might have a series of jobs or do several related things at once. Here are some examples:

- John's mission has to do with transformation. As a search consultant he helps clients to transform their businesses by recruiting senior executives. Occasionally he also invests in them. Since co-writing *Brand You*, he has begun to speak at conferences and to assist people in formulating strategies for their brands. All of these activities involve helping people to transform themselves and their organisations.

- David's mission is reflected in his enthusiasm for developing people. He works with individuals, groups and organisations during periods of rapid change. David helps people to manage their careers and optimise their performance. He trains them in groups and leads exercises for teams, including boards of directors.

- One of David's clients is an IT consultant whose purpose involves solving problems. She is happiest when solving a difficult problem in a complex organisation. Her mission also comes across in her leisure pursuits – she is an accomplished bridge player.

Understanding your mission

Once you understand your mission, it is much easier to decide what you are – and are not – going to do. You will then have more energy for the things you love to do. It also makes life much more enjoyable. You will be on your way to fulfilling your potential.

For example, you might face a decision about a job or business opportunity. Ask yourself: 'Does this fit my mission? Am I here to do this?' You should get a clear yes or no in reply. If the answer is yes, it is worth investigating the opportunity further. If the answer is no, you can politely decline.

You may find yourself in the following situation: you have succeeded in one role and are considering what to do next; you are presented with an opportunity that uses all of your talents but is very similar to your last job. Do you want to go back to that? Is the role sufficiently energising? Will it fire you up? Is it a challenge you cannot resist, or will you just end up achieving more of the same goals? Do you feel trapped by the suggestion that this is all you can do? If you find yourself in a situation like this, it helps to pay attention to how you *feel*. Does the opportunity resonate with you? Does it feel right for you, or are you simply scared of looking beyond it?

We never tell people that a particular job or business is right for them – only they can know. Sometimes it is better to leave the question unanswered, at least for a while. As Lao Tsu said: 'To know that you do not know is the best.' The answer is most likely to come to you when you are relaxed and thinking about nothing in particular. You could be lying in the bath or going for a walk in the countryside. It helps to be away from crowds, buildings and traffic. Some people find that meditation empties their minds of distracting thoughts and emotions. The way forward suddenly becomes clear. It may be a feeling about what you should do next. Some people describe it as an inner voice, telling them which way to go.

Many people find their sense of purpose becomes clearer over time, as they learn more about themselves. By trying different activities you can identify themes that resonate for you. Even an unsuitable job or business can be valuable. It shows you what you *do not* enjoy or do well.

We know a hedge fund manager who was offered a lucrative role in New York. He turned it down in favour of a 12-week cookery course that he had dreamed of doing for some time. This led him to realise that he needed variety and an outlet for his creativity. He wanted to be entrepreneurial and build up a business, without the need to conform to the structure and processes of a large financial institution. He subsequently joined a smaller hedge fund part time, doing what he enjoys and does well. He is still looking for companies to invest in, particularly those that will fit with his values.

With a clear sense of purpose, you can set some goals that are aligned with them. You can also formulate plans and make a list of the tasks that you will need to carry out. In many cases things fall into place without too much planning.

One of David's goals was to write a book that would help to develop people he had either met briefly or might never meet. One day he took part in a treasure hunt and was paired up with John, who had written other books and suggested they write this one together. The book you are reading fulfils one of David's goals, as well as one of John's.

Each of your goals will lead you to an action plan. It might include getting up early every day to write another 500 words for your book. Your action plan will consist of a series of tasks. Some of them will be mundane. If you are a doctor, for example, one of your tasks will be to wash or disinfect your hands between patients to avoid spreading germs. However, since this task is aligned with your purpose/mission, it will be meaningful for you.

Now that you have an understanding of your mission, it is time to have a look at your purpose. The following exercise will help you.

Exercise H: A thousand times your income

We have some news for you. A distant relative, whom you have never even heard of, has died and left you a thousand times the amount of money you normally earn in a year. However, there is one condition: you have to spend all of it on yourself. You have four minutes to write down exactly how you will spend it.

(Four minutes later) There is a second instalment to the bequest, for the same amount. However, this time you are not allowed to spend any of it on yourself, only on other people. How will you spend it? You have three minutes to write it all down.

(Three minutes later) The final clause in the will states that once you have completed the two steps described above, you will be given unlimited money for ever and be granted eternal life. Now that you have unlimited time and money, what will you do? You have two minutes to write it down. Please note that your friends and relatives remain mortal.

Now go back and read what you have written. What are the themes that emerge? What do they say about you? What is stopping you from doing what you want to do *now?* Are you using money as an excuse for not doing it? What could you do differently from now on? Is there a way of doing what you want without vast sums of money?

Look at the results of this exercise compared with what you wrote about talents on pages 31 and 36 and about values on pages 38–40. What are the links between these exercises? There are usually common themes. Are there any clues to your purpose? What is the *essence* of the work you do best? What do you do? How do you do it? What is the *context* in which you do it?

Looking back at what you have written as your mission statement, does this exercise add anything or focus your statement in any way?

Adapted from Life\Work Design, Crystal Barkley Corporation

Henry and Elizabeth

This is what Henry and Elizabeth wrote:

A distant relative has left you a thousand times the amount of money you normally earn in a year. You have to spend all of it on yourself.

Henry found this exercise difficult. Eventually he wrote the following:

- Learn to fly. Buy a Spitfire for fun and a Learjet 31 for travelling the world.

- A Honda Fireblade motorcycle.

- An old house by the sea with a paddock and a horse or two, as well as a house/horse keeper.

- Art nouveau furniture.

- A private box at Chelsea Football Club.

- Holidays around the world, going to all the places I have ever wanted to visit.

- Intensive music lessons on the banjo and the guitar.

- Scuba diving equipment and lessons.

Elizabeth found it much easier. Her list included:

- A personal shopper for a week's indulgence in London and Paris.

- The latest mobile phone and Apple Mac computer.

- An apartment in the centre of London.

- Tickets to any theatre/ballet/opera I want to go to.

- Singing lessons.

- Dance lessons.

- A holiday walking to the North Pole.

- Another holiday in Mauritius to recover!

- A trip to Sotheby's to buy some jewellery and paintings.

- A small château in France.

- Some intensive French lessons to become fluent.

- Some modern art.

- An interior design course.

- Possibly a course in psychodrama.

This time you must spend all of the money on other people.

They both found this relatively easy. Here is Henry's list:

- Set up a children's hospice.

- Set up a fund to give young homeless people a more positive future.

- Give to other charities that help people to learn and apply useful skills, such as computing.

- Make my parents' home easier for them to live in as they get older.

- Give all my relations whatever they need most.

- Help fund children's sports in my area.

- See what has happened to the project I worked on in East Africa and give them something they need for the future.

Elizabeth's thoughts were:

- Give money to my husband to develop his business as he wants.

- Buy new bikes for the girls.

- Air tickets for the family to visit relations in Australia.

- Get a full-time carer to help my mother look after my father, who has senile dementia.

- Build an extension to my parents' house so we can look after dad better.

- Invest money for the hospice I have supported all my life, to pay for extra counselling for the families and more nursing staff.

- Set up drama courses in my area for young people.

- Give money to Oxfam and Greenpeace.

You have been granted eternal life and unlimited money. What will you do? Your friends and relatives remain mortal.

Initially Henry found it difficult to consider eternal life without the people he loved. However, David explained it was an important exercise to help him forget goals and identify his purpose. Henry understood and then wrote the following:

- Do more to find a partner for the first lifetime – someone with whom I have some common values. He realised he was looking for perfection in his partner. This exercise helped him to realise which qualities were really important.

- Consider becoming an expert in some form of conservation, possibly water.

- Keep abreast of developments that might affect the human race and its survival.

- Ride a lot and become a champion in dressage.

- Decide every 50 years which new subject I can excel in and where in the world I will be based.

- Become an expert guitar and banjo player.

Elizabeth was also not sure she wanted eternal life. It was bad enough seeing her father degenerating slowly. However, she wrote down the following thoughts:

- Work in drama, helping people to express themselves better.

- Develop fundraising skills. Work in every aspect of sales, marketing and fundraising, so I can be even more effective.

- Set up research into degenerative diseases.

- Train in animal husbandry and self-sufficiency so I can advise on and promote it.

- Spend time with innovation centres around the world looking for new ways of solving the world's problems.

- Learn to paint.

- Become an architect.

Is there a way of doing what you want to do now without vast quantities of money?

As is often the case, Henry realised that a lot of the things he wanted were within his reach now:

- He could learn to fly. He might not be able to afford a plane of his own, but he could still qualify as a pilot.

- He could also buy the motorbike he wanted, second hand.

- The old house by the sea was too expensive right now but he could rent one in the summer.

- He could continue to collect art nouveau furniture gradually.

- He could support his favourite football team, Chelsea, without the private box.

- He could still visit all the places he wanted to around the world, whenever he had sufficient money and holidays.

- Intensive music lessons were eminently possible. He decided to investigate and ended up learning the banjo.

- The following year he visited Thailand and went scuba diving for the first time.

- He found out about a charity that helps young homeless people. He started giving computer training once a fortnight and identified ways to raise money for new computers.

- He also got in touch with the project he had helped many years earlier in East Africa and started to investigate how he could help.

Elizabeth also saw that some of her desires were reachable without enormous sums of money:

- Her husband Bob gave her a day with a personal shopper for her birthday, plus £500 to spend.

- The latest mobile phone and iPad were affordable.

- Although the apartment in the centre of London was too expensive, she realised that friends who lived there were happy to go with her to the theatre. If she arranged the tickets, they would provide the overnight accommodation. This became a monthly occurrence.

- She did not take up singing lessons, but she and Bob started going to ballroom dancing lessons every week.

- A holiday walking to the North Pole was possible. After some fitness tests she realised she needed surgery. However, after that she did go for a holiday in Mauritius to recover!

- She did not buy jewellery, paintings or modern art at Sotheby's, but she did go to weekly French lessons.

What are the links between these exercises? Are there any clues to your purpose? What is the *essence* of the work you do best? *How* do you do it? What is the *context* in which you do it?

Henry saw several themes in terms of his motivation and relationships. He enjoyed making things run smoothly and helping people to fulfil their potential. Although he did not exactly enjoy public speaking, he realised he could be persuasive and charismatic when he believed in a particular course of action. He was courageous and prepared to take risks when he really believed in something. He knew he could use IT to solve a particular business problem that the software development team had been unable to resolve. They were surprised when he proposed a solution that worked. However, Henry realised that he did not want to take *physical* risks. Riding a motorbike was more of a dream than something he really wanted to do. When he really thought about it, the same was true of learning to fly.

As far as he could tell, his purpose had to do with helping people to fulfil their potential and work together harmoniously. This pervaded his professional and charitable work, his horse riding and his relationships.

Elizabeth realised she was more open with people than she had thought, and was not afraid to make a fool of herself. She had no need to be an expert, even though she was in some respects. Her key thoughts related to determination. She was good at getting what she wanted. The more difficult the task, the more she would go for it. What she enjoyed was the challenge of winning. The salary and bonuses were very important to her in terms of visible reward for her effort. In the longer term she saw herself as a chief executive.

Completing these exercises made Henry and Elizabeth's priorities much clearer to them. Henry realised that he had been looking for the wrong kind of partner in his personal life. Above all, he needed someone who shared his values, so he could build a harmonious relationship. Elizabeth realised that she liked being the centre of attention, building something that would last. She also enjoyed looking after other people in a constructive way. Building something for the future came up as a theme in everything she did, from relationships to business.

Achieving wealth and happiness

Richard Branson, the founder of the Virgin empire, once said: 'I never went into business to make money – but I have found that, if I have fun, the money will come.' In other words, money is not a purpose in itself. If you pursue your purpose then money may be a by-product of what you do and the way you do it.

Think of people you know who are highly successful. Our experience is that most of them love what they do. Whether or not they express it in those terms, they exude energy in their work and when they talk about it. Warren Buffett, arguably the world's most successful investor, said at the Berkshire Hathaway annual meeting in 1988: 'Money is a by-product of doing something I like doing extremely well.' He added: 'I enjoy the process far more than the proceeds, although I have learned to live with those also.'

Some people think they *should* be passionate about their work. However, it remains an intellectual idea rather than a feeling. Both of us have interviewed people who said they were passionate but had zero enthusiasm. If you are honest about how you feel, it is easier to identify your purpose.

Despite all this, you may conclude that you are doing your job or running your business purely to make money. If so, it helps to realise that money is a *goal*. The question is, what does money do for you? Why are you making money? What is the purpose? Once you have a better understanding of your purpose, you will enjoy your work more. Other people will enjoy it more, too. You may make even more money.

If you focus on money alone, your colleagues and customers will probably realise and find you unattractive. However, some of them *will* be attracted if you have a strong sense of purpose and love what you do. This will inevitably bring you more money.

Communicating your mission and purpose

The exterior of a building usually provides some clues to its purpose. There may be a logo that you recognise, perhaps even a slogan. The colour and texture of the surfaces can give you a feel for what goes on inside. Once you enter the building, the ground floor usually tells you a lot more. The people on reception dress and speak in a certain way. There may be a logo with a mission statement, and perhaps some brochures or a television screen explaining what the organisation does. You can also get a feel for the culture from the furniture and any exhibits, paintings or sculptures. There may be rock music from an advertising campaign, or soothing classical music to keep everyone calm while they wait for their appointments.

Sometimes people are described as 'comfortable in their own skin'. Frequently they have a sense of purpose and attract others who are also authentic. They may even say they feel 'at one with the world'.

When you pursue your mission/purpose, you will naturally communicate it. Other people will understand what you do. Those who want what you do – in the way that you do it – will be attracted to you. You will also attract people who believe in your mission and want to help you pursue it.

7

Using archetypes to develop your brand

By now you will have spent some time thinking about your talents, values and purpose. Our next topic is your *brand identity*, which expresses all of them. It consists of the symbols, signs, language, images and colours that distinguish you from other people in your line of work. This brings us back to what David Ogilvy said about advertisers. They should build 'sharply defined personalities for their brands and stick to those personalities year after year. It is the total personality of the brand rather than any trivial product difference that decides its position in the market place'. A distinct, authentic brand identity will help you attract the right employers, clients and colleagues. It will also help them recommend you to others.

The power of archetypes

Archetypes can give your brand a clear meaning, by communicating *how* you do things. The Greek root of the word *archetype* means *first-moulded*. Psychologist Carl Jung believed that we have a universal shared unconscious out of which archetypes emerge as forms or images that everyone recognises. These forms or images have the same meaning for people around the world. We instinctively recognise archetypes in ourselves, other people, objects, situations and organisations, whether or not we are aware that we are doing so.

In 2001, Margaret Mark and Carol S. Pearson published *The Hero and the Outlaw – Building Extraordinary Brands through the Power of Archetypes*. They showed how Jungian archetypes enabled companies to manage the *meaning* of branded products and services. They also suggested that archetypes could be applied to *personal* brands, which is what we will do in this book.

Archetypes can be extremely powerful. We have presented this material to audiences of many nationalities. They all recognise the same archetypes.

We can learn a lot from leading actors and musicians. As Mark and Pearson point out: 'Superstars in the film and entertainment industry, and the agents who manage them, understand that their continued popularity does not hinge simply on the quality or success of the films they make or the visibility they attain. Rather, it depends on creating, nourishing and continuously reinterpreting a unique and compelling identity or "meaning".' Whatever your line of work, you can use a similar approach.

How archetypes work

Our starting point is that you have a purpose. Developing a powerful brand involves *projecting* your purpose to the outside world. Archetypes can help you do this by representing your purpose in a form that everyone recognises. If your behaviour is consistent with your natural archetype(s), your brand will take on a meaning that increases your appeal to people who want what you have to offer.

Below is a description of the archetypes in Mark and Pearson's model. We have modified the titles and used international examples where possible. As you read the paragraphs below, one may stand out as *your* archetype. Others may fit someone you know. Please note that we do not expect you to fit into a box or *become* any of the archetypes below. Instead, you evoke the archetype in your work. The verb *to evoke* is derived from the Latin verb *evocare*, meaning *to call forth*. When you evoke an archetype, your behaviour and the way you present yourself call it forth in the minds of other people and yourself. We will come back to the question of *how* you do this. In the meantime, here are the archetypes. You may notice that some are prevalent in certain occupations but not others.

The Caregiver

The Caregiver archetype is altruistic – motivated by a desire to help others and protect them from harm. Examples include

Mother Teresa, Florence Nightingale and a caring mother or father. Johnson & Johnson, the healthcare company, evokes this archetype, as do private healthcare organisations such as BUPA. Doctors, nurses and social workers often evoke the Caregiver. So do outplacement consultants who help unemployed executives to find a new job. Within a large company, a learning and development director could evoke this archetype.

The Creator

The Creator archetype is often seen in writers, artists, composers, inventors and entrepreneurs. They have daydreams and flashes of inspiration which they translate into reality. The Creator is about self-expression, rather than fitting in. When the Creator archetype is active in people, they often feel *compelled* to create or innovate. They have a vision that must take physical form, and they want to create something of lasting value. Examples include Leonardo da Vinci and Wolfgang Amadeus Mozart. More recent Creators include the American artist Georgia O'Keeffe, Steve Jobs, the co-founder of Apple, and James Dyson, the entrepreneur and inventor of the bagless vacuum cleaner.

The Explorer

The Explorer – unsurprisingly – wants to explore. Explorers want to maintain independence. They are naturally curious about everything. There is an underlying feeling of dissatisfaction and restlessness. The exploration can be geographical, as it was for Christopher Columbus, Marco Polo and *Star Trek*. However, the joy of discovery can also extend to new products and services. Explorers have an underlying desire to find out what fits with their inner needs and preferences. The actor Ewan McGregor evokes the Explorer in his motorcycle journeys and aftershave advertisements. Richard Branson evokes the Explorer when he travels thousands of miles in a hot-air balloon or invests millions in an emerging sector of the economy. Francis Crick and James Watson, the molecular biologists, evoked the Explorer when they discovered the structure of DNA.

The Hero

The Hero acts courageously to improve a situation. They are attracted to chaos because it provides an opportunity for heroism. Heroes stand up for what they believe in. There are fictional heroes such as Superman and James Bond. Real-life examples include Nelson Mandela and Aung San Suu Kyi, the Burmese dissident who has spent much of her life under house arrest. Amelia Earhart evoked the Hero when she became the first woman to fly solo across the Atlantic. The police, ambulance drivers and firefighters can also evoke the Hero. Some executives do so when they turn a company around and prevent it from going into liquidation. They may even describe potential disasters in detail to those around them. It adds to the thrill of pulling through and making everything right.

Returning to our example in Chapter 1, here is some online commentary from Tokyo Newsline: 'Carlos Ghosn, the ambassador of change, the icebreaker, *le cost killer*, the troubleshooter, or however you wish to refer to him, is Japan's hero. He has provided a glimmer of hope to leaders of thousands of ailing corporations who are desperately seeking solutions to their problems ... Since arriving in Japan, Ghosn has taken Nissan from the brink of bankruptcy to a profit-making entity in just two years.'

The Innocent

The Innocent is about fostering purity and goodness. The Latin and Old French root of the word *innocent* means 'no harm'. The primary aim is happiness, perhaps even the experience of paradise. Innocent Drinks was founded in 1999 and now sells more than 2 million smoothies each week. The ingredients are fruit and fruit juice, with no 'weird stuff' – in other words, artificial ingredients. Examples from Hollywood include Tom Hanks in the role of Forrest Gump. Disney evokes the Innocent in films such as *Bambi* and *Snow White*. A dietician or someone who helps you stop smoking could also evoke this archetype. Monks, nuns and holy people in many cultures evoke the Innocent. This archetype is also known as the Child.

Some business people evoke the Innocent, at least for a while. One example was Anita Roddick when she founded The Body Shop, which now sells natural skin- and hair-care products in over 50 countries.

The Jester

On the surface the Jester usually has a good time, enjoying the moment. However, they often have something important to say. The Jester gets bored easily and is happy breaking the rules. This archetype can suit consumer brands such as Ben & Jerry's ice-cream company. Fun and humour pervade the brand's activities, including its campaign to help combat global warming: 'Ben & Jerry's Climate Change College is a launch pad for 18–30 year olds who agree with us that ice caps, just like ice cream, are best kept frozen.'

Jesters say things that others dare not say, and can be highly influential. Personal assistants sometimes play this role. Jesters also provoke other people, exposing their prejudices. Sacha Baron Cohen did this as Borat in the film *Cultural Learnings of America for Make Benefit Glorious Nation of Kazakhstan*.

One of our former colleagues is the co-founder of a successful consulting firm. He attributes his success to playing the role of the Jester: 'Clients like being challenged. They also want to compare themselves. However, I have to be discreet. Much of what I do goes on behind the curtain. If I find out they are doing something new in the US, I send them a message right away, to suggest I help them do the same thing in Europe. I win lots of business by crossing the bridge to their castle and gently provoking them.'

The Lover

The Lover wants to find and give love, and experience sensual pleasure. This archetype is concerned with staying close to the people, surroundings and activities you love. There is an archetypal yearning for true love in many Hollywood stars. It is also seen in products such as perfume, chocolate and ice cream. Fashion models, pop stars and writers of popular fiction often evoke the Lover.

One of the most famous business people to evoke the Lover is Coco Chanel, who was known both as a dress designer and as the mistress of famous and wealthy men. Sales of her perfume, Chanel No. 5, rocketed once it received the free endorsement of Marilyn Monroe. Chanel had a keen sense of her personal brand. When asked why she did not marry the Duke of Westminster, she replied: 'There have been several Duchesses of Westminster. There is only one Chanel.'

The Magician

The role of the Magician is to *transform*. One of the underlying themes is discovering the laws of the universe in order to make things happen. The Magician pays attention to hunches and meaningful coincidences. Harry Potter, the star of the eponymous novels, is one example.

Another example of this archetype is Paulo Coelho's best-selling fable, *The Alchemist*. The Magician often appears in advertisements for cleaning products, with tag-lines such as 'Bang! And the dirt is gone!'. For many people, Steve Jobs evokes the Magician. At Apple he constantly had ideas that transformed people's lives. He was sometimes described as 'The Wizard of Cupertino'.

A plastic surgeon could evoke the Magician, as could a finance director who specialises in floating companies on the stock market, transforming them from private companies into public ones.

The Ordinary Guy/Girl

Ordinary Guys and Girls are OK as they are. They want to fit in and connect with others. Entertainers such as Bruce Springsteen in the US and Robbie Williams in the UK evoke this archetype. In the corporate world it is seen in executives who have *the common touch*. Ordinary Guys and Girls enjoy self-deprecating humour, demonstrating that they do not take themselves too seriously. They often watch popular sports and have a connection with people that crosses social boundaries. Successful sales people frequently evoke the Ordinary Guy or Girl. When they first make contact with an organisation that could buy their product or service, they chat and build rapport with people at all levels, from the receptionist to the office manager and the boss's personal assistant. This helps every stage of the sales process to go smoothly.

Stelios Haji-Ioannou, the founder of easyJet and many other businesses, illustrates the fact that you *evoke* an archetype rather than *become* it. Despite his wealthy upbringing, he is known for giving the man and woman in the street what they want at an affordable price. Having made his name with his low-cost airline, his subsequent ventures include easyCruise, easyCar, easyHotel and easyOffice.

The Outlaw

The Outlaw is a maverick who rebels and breaks the rules. They disrupt the status quo. Outlaw brands include The Rolling Stones, Madonna and Jack Nicholson. For many years Apple Computer evoked the Outlaw. Its logo of an apple with a bite taken out of it recalls Adam and Eve, who ate the forbidden fruit and were cast out of the Garden of Eden. In the early days this was aligned with Apple's role as the computer manufacturer that challenged the Ruler, namely IBM. Apple remains the preferred option for many 'black-collar' workers such as graphic designers and other creative people. It reinforces the distinction between themselves and the 'suits' who rule the companies where they work.

Entrepreneurs often evoke the Outlaw. They break with convention in order to start something new. One example is Niklas Zennström, co-founder of Kazaa and Skype. At Kazaa he pioneered peer-to-peer file-sharing on the internet, resulting in a legal battle with the music industry over breach of copyright. His public profile helped him launch Skype, a service offering free phone calls that became a threat to established telecoms companies.

The Ruler

The Ruler takes control, creating order out of chaos. Rulers *have* to organise things. Alexander the Great evoked this archetype, as did Margaret Thatcher when she was Britain's prime minister. The Ruler wants to create a successful and prosperous family, company or other organisation, but fears being overthrown. SAP, the German software company, evokes the Ruler by helping people who run large organisations to keep things under control.

The Ruler is often seen in commercial buildings with Doric columns that recall ancient Greece and the Roman Empire. Accountants, finance directors and chief financial officers often evoke the Ruler. They help to keep business empires under control.

The Sage

The Sage helps people to understand their world. Plato and Confucius both evoked the Sage. Some universities do so, too. They project the message that by studying there you will gain a deeper understanding. Some companies, such as McKinsey, also embody this archetype by hiring highly educated people and training them in a particular way. McKinsey also publishes a journal, *The McKinsey Quarterly*. In a software company, the head of software development sometimes evokes the Sage. If they are highly knowledgeable rather than sales-oriented, it is reassuring for both customers and shareholders. Another example of the Sage is Edward De Bono, the author of 62 books including *Lateral Thinking*. The Sage archetype is also known as the Wise Man/Woman.

Identifying your archetypes

As we said earlier, none of us fits neatly into a box. During the course of a day you might evoke the Caregiver, the Hero, the Ruler, the Jester, the Creator and the Lover. However, you are likely to be naturally inclined towards one archetype in your work. You will feel attracted to it. People who know you well will recognise it in you. You will build a much stronger brand if you evoke one archetype – or possibly two – consistently. Consciously or unconsciously, people want to know what you stand for. They also value consistency. If you consistently evoke a particular archetype, they will feel they know who you are and can trust you to behave in a certain way. They will feel safe around you. They will know what they can ask you to do, if the need arises. All this makes it easier for them to choose you or recommend you to others.

As we mentioned earlier, you *evoke* an archetype rather than become it. Charles is a fund manager who works mainly on his own, with a handful of colleagues, and does not *lead* anyone. However, the archetype he evokes is the Ruler. This is not because *he* is a ruler but because those who *want to rule* turn to him for help.

His ultimate boss has a large fortune that he wishes to protect, along with his family and the empire he rules. If Charles wants to keep his job and be well rewarded, it makes sense to ensure that everything he says and does at work is consistent with the Ruler archetype. If he begins to evoke the Jester or the Outlaw, for example, his boss may soon feel uncomfortable.

The Ruler is by no means the only archetype open to fund managers. Some of them evoke the Hero. They take risks and succeed against the odds. Sometimes they produce impressive returns. Occasionally they incur enormous losses. However, investors like Charles's boss have little appetite for heroism. They want to rule their empires and maintain stability.

Life would be simpler if each of us needed to evoke only one archetype consistently at work. However, many people naturally evoke two of them. Here are some examples:

- Henry, whom we introduced earlier, evokes both the Ruler and the Caregiver. He helps the bank's top management to keep things under control. At the same time he helps his staff to develop skills that will enable them to progress in their careers.

- The chief executive of a large media company evokes the Ordinary Guy when he builds relationships with his staff, including journalists, sales people, creatives and others from a wide range of backgrounds. He evokes the Magician while he is transforming the company, helping it to succeed in a new environment.

- A business development director employed by another large company evokes the Explorer while she searches for suitable businesses to acquire. She also evokes the Creator when she draws up plans to launch new ventures in-house.

- A doctor evokes the Magician when he prescribes medicine that helps people recover from sudden illnesses. He evokes the Caregiver when he recommends changes in their diet and lifestyle that will protect them from relapses.

- Michael Moore, the film-maker and social critic, evokes the Jester and the Outlaw. He says things that many people do not want to hear. He gets away with it because he does so with humour.

- Another comedian evokes the Jester and the Ordinary Guy when he makes jokes about himself and his circumstances.

People relate to him and his background. They see themselves in him, so they laugh at his predicament – and their own.

■ Barack Obama evoked the Ordinary Guy and the Hero when he campaigned to become president of the United States in 2008. His campaign successfully emphasised his upbringing in a broken home. The financial crisis helped him to evoke the Hero at a time when voters were already looking for someone who would save them from disaster.

Madonna: a case study in combining two archetypes

Madonna is the highest-earning female singer of all time, having sold over 200 million albums. She was the third of six children born to Italian–American parents. Madonna's father worked in the Chrysler car factory near Detroit. Her mother died when Madonna was six and she was brought up as a Roman Catholic, which has strongly influenced her music and her imagery. She has both acknowledged and rebelled against her religion throughout her career.

Madonna has followed David Bowie's example by continuously changing her image, thus maintaining people's interest in her. However, in terms of archetypes she has consistently evoked both the Lover and the Outlaw. As she once said: 'When I was tiny my grandmother used to beg me not to go with boys, to love Jesus and be a good girl. I grew up with two images of women: the Virgin and the whore.'

In the 1980s a generation of young women identified with her as someone who fought her way to the top in a man's world while managing to remain rebellious and sexy. By marketing herself as a sex symbol she attracted attention from a male audience at the same time. Some of the key events in her career show how she has built a powerful brand:

■ Her strong style enabled her to cross boundaries between audiences. Her music is played in both gay and straight clubs in the United States and appeals to a variety of ethnic groups.

- The launch of MTV, the 24-hour music TV channel, and its imitators helped her to reach a much larger audience than would have been possible through touring alone. In early 1985 her second album and video *Like A Virgin* made her a fixture on MTV. Video enabled her to control her image carefully and occasionally borrow ideas from Hollywood films, inviting comparison with film stars of the past.

- She recorded other people's songs as well as her own, which helped her to produce high-quality work consistently.

- In 1990, sales of her compilation album *The Immaculate Collection* were boosted by the furore over the video of *Justify My Love,* which was banned by MTV and swiftly became a must-have item. By February 1991 it had become the first video short to sell more than 400,000 copies.

- In the summer of 2006 she became the worldwide face of H&M, the clothing retailer, launching her own fashion line, *M by Madonna,* in March 2007.

- In 2008, *Billboard* magazine ranked Madonna at number two, behind *The Beatles,* on the *Billboard Hot 100 All-Time Top Artists,* making her the most successful solo artist in the history of the *Billboard* chart.

Source: *Madonna – the Complete Guide to Her Music*, by Rikky Rooksby (Omnibus Press)

As far as archetypes are concerned, the main thing is to identify one or two that suit you best – that attract you and make you feel most comfortable. Each of us draws upon other archetypes at various times. It does not matter, provided you are authentic. In other words, you consistently act in accordance with your values.

For example, John usually evokes the Magician in his work. His aim is to help people transform their businesses and their careers. However, when he recruits chief executives, finance directors or chairmen, he also evokes the Ruler. When he writes books he evokes the Magician and the Creator. As a consultant, David works with a wide range of organisations. Although he is most comfortable evoking the Magician or the Caregiver, he sometimes needs to evoke the Outlaw or the Jester for a specific reason.

Distinguishing your archetypes

You do not have to evoke the same archetype(s) as the organisation where you work. For example, we know an all-day café that evokes the Innocent. The ingredients are pure and fresh. The Italian flat bread is baked on site. However, the founder embodies both the Innocent and the Creator. While he develops the recipes himself – and safeguards the purity of the brand – this is his third start-up. One day he plans to spend more time on creative writing. It helps that his investors see both the Innocent and the Creator in him. They realise that he is intent on creating a profitable business as well as baking nice bread.

Archetypes are not on a spectrum with two extremes, or a wheel consisting of opposites. Archetypes are simply different and each of us evokes them all at some point. At the same time, we are attracted to certain archetypes that fit us best. It may, therefore, be useful to work for an organisation that evokes an archetype which is also prominent in you. For example, if your talents are in financial analysis and the Ruler archetype fits you well, you would probably find it satisfying to work for a Ruler-type organisation, such as a bank. However, it is worth bearing in mind that different departments within the organisation have a secondary archetype that relates to the work being done there. For example, the marketing department of a Caregiver insurance company might adopt a Jester approach to its advertising in a highly competitive market.

Here is a summary of the archetypes we have discussed in this book:

The Caregiver	Helps and protects from harm
The Creator	Compelled to create and innovate
The Explorer	Explores and discovers
The Hero	Acts courageously to put things right
The Innocent	Seeks purity, goodness and happiness
The Jester	Has a good time but may convey a serious message
The Lover	Finds and gives love and sensual pleasure
The Magician	Transforms situations
The Ordinary Guy/Girl	OK as they are; connects with others
The Outlaw	Rebels and breaks the rules
The Ruler	Takes control; creates order out of chaos
The Sage	Helps people to understand their world

It is now time to identify *your* archetype(s). The following exercise will help you.

Exercise I: Your archetype(s)

Refer to the results of the exercises that you have recently completed in Chapters 5 and 6. Take another look at your top five values, your mission and your purpose. Do they suggest an archetype that you evoke naturally? Show the description of the archetypes on pages 71–8 to five colleagues and/or friends. Include people you have known for a short while. Ask them which archetype(s) they can identify in you. If you and they pick the same archetype(s), then you have a clear brand identity. If they pick a range of different archetypes, it means your brand is not yet clearly defined.

Henry and Elizabeth

Henry realised that he evoked both the Ruler and the Caregiver. He is trusted and respected by the bank's top management. They count on him to manage and control projects successfully. It helps them to rule. At the same time he helps his staff to develop new skills, so they can progress in their careers. He is committed to helping those who need support, thereby evoking the Caregiver. He prefers to work quietly, building his arguments on strong logical foundations, ensuring that the strategy fits the needs of the staff, the management and the shareholders.

Elizabeth was attracted to the Hero archetype above all others. She feels she works best that way and enjoys the challenge of doing things better than ever before. If a business is underperforming, she takes great pleasure in making rapid improvements. She also evokes the Creator, with her emphasis on building lasting relationships and robust organisations.

You may be tempted to keep your options open by giving different messages to different people. However, by trying to appeal to everyone, you can fail to appeal strongly to *anyone.* Think of washing powder in your local supermarket. Some brands wash whiter than white; others keep your colours bright; some are designed to protect people with allergies. Each has a unique appeal. One will stand out as the best for the purpose you have in mind, while others blend into the background. No one wants a washing powder that may perhaps be quite good for something or other.

Many of us face too many choices and have to process too much information. Strong brands simplify our decisions and give us a feeling of certainty. In most product categories the majority of people can remember only two or three leading brands. In cola beverages, it could be Coke, Pepsi and …? The same applies to people who are considering using your services. The clearer the image of what you do and what you stand for, the easier it will be for them to choose *you*. Once you have identified the archetype you evoke *naturally*, it is important to do so *consistently* in the eyes of your target market. You should be the first or second person they think of whenever they have a need. Many people want a choice of supplier, but they do not need more than two or three to choose from. Make sure you are one of them!

Your brand identity is like the exterior and interior of a building – they tell people what it is for and how things are done there. When you walk into a bank with Doric columns made of granite, you will probably have a feeling of solidity and security. The building evokes the Ruler, giving the impression that your savings are likely to be safe there. When someone walks into a health food store, they see the nuts, seeds and dried fruit in simple packaging. They notice the stripped pine shelving. The surroundings evoke the Innocent.

It is important for you to evoke your archetype consistently in everything you do and in all your presentation material. That way people will know what you stand for and will feel safe with you.

Chapter

8

Staying focused

Once you know your main archetype you can seek opportunities to evoke it. This will help you focus on your purpose and avoid being distracted. If your brand is a building then each successful project adds a storey. It will gradually become a landmark.

Jobs, businesses and short-term contracts are *vehicles* for pursuing your purpose. It is important to choose the right vehicle for you. However, some people apply for any job they have the faintest chance of getting. They risk ending up in a role that does not suit them. It is better to steer clear of employers who do not want what you enjoy doing most. You will save everyone a lot of time and trouble.

Focusing on your purpose and your archetype gives you scope to move around and change roles if necessary. Those who lose their jobs may look for something similar, but they could also consider extending their brands into a related field. People who know them will see this as a logical step.

It takes courage to focus on your purpose and your archetype. However, it is much more rewarding than randomly pestering people for a job. Knowing your purpose makes it easier to spot opportunities that are right for you. It also helps you to ask the right questions and find out whether the culture fits your way of working. The clearer you are about what you want, the more likely you are to get it. Your thoughts, feelings and actions will send out a consistent message.

Choosing customers and projects

Whether you are employed or self-employed, it is worth considering the effect that each new customer or client will have on your brand. Sales people are remembered for winning a particular contract that boosted their company or threatened its survival. Bankers, advertising executives, public relations consultants and headhunters are all judged by the clients they represent. If the work itself fills you with enthusiasm, you are likely to do an excellent job and strengthen your brand.

However, some people take on work they find uninspiring, feeling they have to prove themselves. Unfortunately, you are what you eat. You will become known for the work you find uninspiring and attract more of the same. You may also discourage people from giving you projects you would find more exciting.

A client of David's is a human resources director who became a self-employed consultant. She planned to focus on highly paid strategic work. Then someone asked her to deal with a complicated bullying case, which she handled as a favour. This led to more of the same. As word spread that she was the expert in bullying, she attracted more problems and less of the work she wanted to do.

Some people take on lots of projects just to keep their plates full. If you are employed, you may have to do this in order to meet your budget and keep your job. However, if the work does not fit your purpose, it can dilute your focus and weaken your brand. If you decline it, you can spend the time saved on activities that will build your brand and increase your revenues. For example, you could speak at a conference or write an article that potential clients will read.

Turning down work can feel like a brave thing to do. However, once you get used to doing what inspires you, you will feel more confident about it. Your state of mind is just as important as your marketing efforts in attracting the work you really want to do.

Respecting your heritage

Personal brands have a lot in common with luxury brands. In both cases customers will pay a premium for top quality, unique features and a distinct brand identity. There is a magic formula for luxury that can also be applied to personal brands. Successful luxury brands combine two attributes: heritage and contemporary appeal. As far as heritage is concerned, they tell you about the craftsmen who have been working away for a century or more. They also underline their contemporary appeal by employing talented designers who tap into the latest trends.

Many unsuccessful luxury brands have one attribute but not both. Some project their heritage, but the design is not contemporary. Customers dismiss these brands as *old-fashioned.* You might inherit one of their products from your grandparents, but you would not buy any of them. Other unsuccessful brands have well-known designers but discard their heritage. Their products have no consistent theme – they just follow fashion. The quality is not great either. The brand becomes *trendy* and ends up competing with other fashion items. It is unable to command a premium. Brands that have neither heritage nor contemporary appeal are *irrelevant* to consumers of luxury goods (see diagram below).

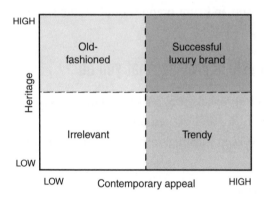

By combining heritage and contemporary appeal, successful luxury brands become far more successful and profitable than those that are old-fashioned or trendy. The same principle applies to your personal brand. Potential employers and clients are reassured by where you worked and what you did earlier in your career. It is part of your heritage. Throughout your working life, colleagues, headhunters, journalists and others will say 'He began his career with ABC company', or 'She practised law before starting a chain of restaurants'. Even if you are now doing something completely different, your heritage gives people an indication of the quality of your work. It has a big impact on how they perceive you. It affects their willingness to buy from you, work with you or invest in your business.

There are two big mistakes to avoid. The first is to discard your heritage. This gives your clients less reassurance, making you less valuable to them. It is even worse to criticise your old firm, particularly if your contract was terminated and you feel sore about it. Negativity is a big turn-off and is bad for your brand.

The second mistake is to stop improving and updating your brand. After a while you lose contemporary appeal and are regarded as old-fashioned. Saying 'When I was at IBM we did it this way' only works for a short time. It is essential to innovate, so that what you are doing now is even better than what you did at IBM. The world moves on. You and your brand should do the same.

Continuously improving what you do

We can all improve the way we serve people. If you are committed to what you do, and excited about it, you will have the energy you need to keep learning, improving and innovating. Your work should be:

1 Top-quality.

2 Distinctive.

3 Consistent with your values and your purpose.

4 Valuable to the people you serve.

What about the quality of your work? If you look carefully you can always find ways to do it better. One example is written documents. Some people speak fluently but write carelessly. Their documents are hard to read and understand. Once they begin to circulate, they damage that person's brand. Think of your written work as an advertisement. If it is succinct and clear, it will enhance your reputation for quality. Imagine you are going to read it aloud on national radio. That will help you to produce a first-class document.

It is important to be distinctive in ways that are consistent with your values and your purpose. This could include any pro bono or voluntary work you do. The Black Eyed Peas' youth academies across the United States encourage underprivileged teenagers to get involved in the arts. Roger Moore, one of the actors who played James Bond, has worked as a UNICEF Goodwill Ambassador. In our earlier examples Henry used his ability to develop people in his voluntary work with homeless people. Elizabeth applied her sales skills to fundraising for a charity. In both cases their voluntary work was consistent with their values and their purpose.

For your work to be valuable to your clients it must meet their needs, some of which may be unspoken. We know a dentist who was one of the first in the UK to offer tooth whitening. He now also offers Botox, based on his knowledge of facial musculature. While few people would walk into a dental surgery looking for that treatment, many have responded to the poster in his waiting room. He knows his patients care about their appearance as well as their health.

If you are a specialist in one area, you can play to your strengths while seizing opportunities in other, related areas. We know a medical doctor who works as a coroner. He has also become a consultant to film directors. He helps them and their special-effects teams to ensure that every illness or injury is true to life.

Asking for feedback

The moment of truth comes when you start working on a project. Some clients and employers will give you feedback as you go along; others prefer to do so once you have finished. You may be reluctant to ask for feedback if you are afraid of criticism. However, it becomes much easier if you are committed to being excellent at what you do.

Imagine you are a food manufacturer testing a new recipe on consumers. Some may loathe your latest concoction. However, if you absorb their feedback and adapt your recipe, they will keep buying from you. Even in difficult situations, feedback can strengthen your relationship if your client senses your commitment. They will have even more reason to keep working with you, since you have shown you are responsive.

Clients of executive search firms are usually impressed if a headhunter admits to a problem and makes strenuous efforts to resolve it. We are not recommending you deliberately create problems. However, they can be an opportunity to demonstrate your values and your commitment to your purpose. Your clients may surprise you by recommending you to other people.

Chapter

9

Explaining what you do

If you have completed the exercises so far, you will be much clearer about your talents, your values, your purpose and your preferred archetype. The next question is, how will you explain what you do?

People often ask, 'What do you do?'. One of the most forbidding answers is, 'How long have you got?'. Your listeners probably have short attention spans and plenty of other things to think about. It is therefore essential to work out your message and put it across clearly, just as you would if you were advertising a product or a business. The aim is to be authentic, concise and memorable – face to face, in print and online.

You may need slightly different messages for different situations. However, they should all fit your purpose and your main archetype.

You have many facets, just like a precious stone. Imagine you are in a dark room. Someone shines a spotlight on you from a particular direction, illuminating some of your facets but not others. Now they move the spotlight and shine it from another direction. Other facets stand out.

It is for you to decide which facets you are going to show to the outside world at any particular time.

Your unique combination of talents, skills and experience

If asked to describe a friend or colleague, most people would say between two and four things about them – usually a mixture of their talents, skills and experience. It is often a rare combination. It may even be unique. If you can identify this combination and state it clearly, it will be easy for people to grasp what you have to offer and then tell others. Many of the best opportunities come through word-of-mouth recommendation.

We discussed your talents in Chapter 4. Now it is time to talk about your skills and experience.

As you apply your talents to your career, you acquire experience and develop certain skills. A given talent could be developed into a variety of skills. For example, a talent for using words could be developed into the skills of a novelist, a translator, an editor, a screenplay writer, a journalist or a stockbroker, among many other occupations. A talent for spotting numerical patterns could be developed into the role of a statistician, a codebreaker, an actuary, an accountant or an investment analyst. You could apply a talent for organising people in the role of a chief executive, an army officer or a concert promoter. The more experience you gain of applying your talents in a particular way, the more valuable you become to employers and clients.

Identifying your skills and experience

It is important that you recognise your skills and experience. The following exercise will help you.

Exercise J: Your skills and experience

Make a list of all the skills and types of experience you have acquired so far. They are likely to be rooted in your talents. The following questions will help you identify them:

- What have you studied?

- In which industries have you worked?

- Which languages do you speak?

- Have you ever spoken in public? To what kind of audience?

- At what stages in an organisation's life have you worked? Examples include start-up, rapid growth, consolidation, decline and liquidation.

■ Which processes have you mastered? Examples include launching a product, auditing a company, curing an addiction through hypnotherapy, renovating a building, writing a book, running a change programme, running a manufacturing process, rewiring a house.

■ What have you achieved that is measurable and could be relevant to a new employer or client?

People who do this exercise often discover something they have overlooked. They also become much clearer about what they have to offer.

Henry and Elizabeth

Henry and Elizabeth will help us to get started. Here are some of Henry's skills and experiences:

■ Degree in history.

■ A senior manager in commercial and investment banking.

■ Boosting efficiency by restructuring divisions within banks.

■ Strong programme-management skills, applying information technology to finance.

■ Creating a computer program that transformed how people work.

■ Identifying how people work and creating processes that fit their needs.

Here are some of Elizabeth's:

■ Degree in business administration from the University of Hong Kong.

■ Former president of the students' union.

- The youngest-ever brand manager at her previous employer, a major food company.

- Strong sales skills.

- Experience of designing websites that increase sales significantly.

- A proven ability to revitalise brands that are flagging.

- Using statistical analysis to support arguments.

- Spotting trends in emerging buying habits and capitalising on them.

Identifying your unique combination

In Exercise A on page 31 we identified your talents. In Exercise J above we identified your skills and experience. Now we will use the results of these two exercises to identify your unique combination of talents, skills and experience. We are looking for the combination that makes you unique *in your environment*. Someone on the other side of the world may have the same combination as you but operate in a different context. Unless both of you do your business entirely electronically, you may not compete with each other directly.

Exercise K: Your unique combination of talents, skills and experience

Choose a talent, skill or type of experience which you feel is one of your strongest. Imagine you are in a circle with everyone in the world who has that particular talent, skill or experience. It may be hundreds, thousands or millions of people. It does not matter.

Now pick another of your talents, skills or experiences. Maybe lots of other people have that, too. You and they are in another big circle which overlaps with the first.

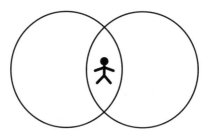

You and a relatively small number of people are in both circles.

Now pick a third talent, skill or experience that you and other people have. If we add a third circle to the diagram, you and an even smaller number of people will have all three talents, skills or experiences.

For example, the first circle might include everyone in the world who has a degree in engineering. The second circle might include everyone who speaks both French and English. The third circle might include everyone who has a talent for finding practical solutions to everyday problems.

Make a list of the 3–6 talents, skills or experiences that, taken together, make you rare if not unique:

1 ....

2 ....

3 ....

4 ....

5 ....

6 ....

Please note that not all the points listed in your unique combination have to be related to your work – it may be something else that makes you different.

When we run seminars we ask the participants to work in pairs. Each person drafts their unique combination and presents it to the other, who edits it. This greatly improves the end result. Everything you say about yourself has to be objective and measurable. The editor rules out vague assertions such as 'I am a leader' or 'I am entrepreneurial'. If you are a leader or an entrepreneur, it should be possible to say something measurable, such as:

■ Led teams of up to 20 expert consultants.

or

■ Founded a retail business whose revenue grew to X million in five years.

It is best to avoid subjective descriptions such as 'a dynamic person'. Some people may think you are dynamic, others may disagree. Likewise, saying you are 'a good communicator' does not help much. Few people would say they were bad communicators!

Most people with a few years' work experience have a unique combination consisting of 4–6 points. You may be unique with only two or three. However, it is best to keep going and consider all of your talents, skills and experience. It helps to do this exercise with someone who knows you well, or at least check the results with them afterwards. Having seen you in different situations, they can have useful insights. They may also realise that you have missed out something that you do naturally and take for granted. For example, you may do something purely for enjoyment which might one day become part of your job or business. Examples include photography, music, teaching and writing.

As we said in Chapter 2, you should not market yourself as the cheapest. Anyone can offer to work for even less. It is better to base your unique combination on attributes that provide a real benefit to someone. If you build a brand that has significant value for other people, you can charge a higher price while retaining loyal customers.

Using your unique combination to market yourself

Once you know your unique combination, you can use it in many ways. For example, you can use it in the Summary section on LinkedIn. It will help people to grasp what you have to offer and find ways of working with you.

Understanding your unique combination is particularly useful when you are looking for a new job, or new clients or customers. It helps you to understand what you have to offer that makes you different. For example, if you are sending your CV to a recruitment firm, it is often helpful if you summarise what you have to offer in 4–6 bullet points, which you can include in your introductory letter or email.

Many executive search firms, or firms of headhunters, use a technique known as an acid test, which summarises the criteria for a particular assignment in 4–6 bullet points. If several of the bullet points in your unique combination match those in the acid test, you may be put on the long list right away, making it much more likely that you will end up on the short list and be offered the job.

If you are writing speculatively to an employer or recruitment consultant, you may not know their exact needs. However, by summarising what you have to offer, you will make it easier for them to choose you if an opportunity arises. You can write a short letter or email along the following lines so readers can see at a glance whether you have the skills and experience they need:

'I can offer you/your clients the following:

- A 15-year track record in software, including 10 years in sales and marketing.

- Experience of leading teams of up to 50 people, based in several countries.

- Five years' experience as the chief executive of a high-growth company.

- A working knowledge of Mandarin.'

You can use your unique combination to extend your activities into new areas that employers, clients or customers will see as a logical progression. Henry did this at one point. He already had a reputation for solving problems within financial institutions. He then applied his knowledge of computers – which had previously been a hobby – to help a bank process information more efficiently. By combining this knowledge with his financial skills, he strengthened his reputation as a problem solver.

A woman working in public relations in the metallurgy sector found she was more excited about promoting individuals than companies. She therefore looked for a new role in which she could focus on what she did best. It was a challenge at first. Her network, including the headhunters she met, saw her as 'a corporate PR executive specialising in metallurgy'.

Your brand often lags way behind what you do now, so it is essential to keep updating people. You may have broadened or deepened your activities, but most of your contacts are probably unaware that you have done so. You can start to expand your business by telling them what you do now, both face to face and online. One of the best ways is to give them concrete examples of work you have done recently. We will discuss this in Chapter 10 when we talk about telling your story.

Summarising what you do in a couple of sentences

Once you understand your unique combination of talents, skills and experience, you can express it even more concisely when you need to, particularly when someone asks, 'What do you do?'.

This is how Henry answers the question: 'I analyse how people interact. Then I create IT solutions to help them overcome business problems quickly and efficiently.'

This is Elizabeth's answer: 'I spot trends. Then I use numbers and practical examples to persuade clients to adopt new ideas that will make money for them.'

Some of us provide more than one service. We therefore need more than one version.

This is what John says, (a) to companies: 'I recruit chief executives, finance directors and chairmen. Where appropriate, I reinvest some of the fee in equity' and (b) to senior executives and professionals:

'We help senior people to formulate personal brand strategies. It helps them to attract customers, clients, staff and investors.'

This is what David says, (a) to companies: 'I help your people to fulfil their potential in ways that improve your bottom line' and (b) to executives: 'I work with you to clarify what you want out of your future and help you achieve it.'

Summarising what you do in three seconds

Sometimes you will need to be even more concise. Imagine you are at a social event. Someone asks what you do. Just when you have begun to answer, you are interrupted by someone who wants you to pass them a plate of food. Then the conversation moves on to another topic.

That person you were talking to could lead you to a great opportunity. It is best to assume that you have only a few seconds to tell them what you do. You therefore need a message that is concise and memorable. We call it your *three-second statement.* If you say only that you are a headhunter, an accountant or a psychiatrist, the conversation may end there. If you mention two activities, at least twice as many people will want to know more. They will pick up on the topic that interests them most.

You can base your three-second statement on your unique combination. If you have already asked the other person a question or two, you can make your statement directly relevant to them. Here are some examples. Each person has chosen two points from their unique combination:

- **'I'm a business psychologist with a marketing background.'**
  'People often ask what a business psychologist is. The link between psychology and marketing is new to most people. Some of them want to explore it. A lot of people are interested in psychology or marketing, or both.'

■ **'I'm a banker and a school governor.'**
'Some people are happy talking about banking, particularly
if they work in financial services. However, a lot more people
have children and talk to me about education. Being a school
governor gives me a link with the local community.'

■ **'I'm the chief executive of a retail business. I'm also on the
board of a private equity fund.'**
'Some people want to talk about retail. Everyone has an
opinion because we all go shopping. Financial people usually
want to talk about private equity.'

■ **'I'm an account director for an advertising agency. I also do a
lot of photography.'**
'Some people want to know which agency I work for. Others
ask what kind of photographs I take. The two work well
together, because so much advertising is visual. Being a
photographer makes me better at advertising, and vice versa.'

■ **'I'm studying journalism. At the moment I'm getting some
work experience.'**
'Many people are interested in journalism. They ask me why
I chose it, how I decide what I'm going to write about, and
so on.'

■ **'I'm an accountant. I focus on helping small businesses.'**
'Being an accountant isn't unusual, but some people have a
tax issue that they ask me about. Many people either know
someone who runs their own business or want to start one
themselves. Either way, we get talking.'

■ **'I'm an electrician. I also play the trumpet in a jazz band.'**
'It's an unusual combination for most people, so they tend to
remember me. There's a trumpet on my business cards and on
the side of my van. My business is called Clarion Electrical.'

■ **'I'm a dentist. Most of my patients are investment bankers.'**
'Most people like to keep away from dentistry as much as
possible, but some are intrigued that I specialise in treating

investment bankers. Other medical people are usually happy to talk about dentistry.'

Your three-second statement helps to communicate your unique combination and make people remember you. For example, there are plenty of dentists, but we know only one who specialises in investment bankers. That makes her unique and memorable.

Exercise L: Your three-second statement

The aim is to catch people's attention and be memorable. Think of two aspects of what you do that could interest other people and are likely to make you unique. Write down one or two sentences, in the style you would use during a casual conversation. Test your three-second statement on friends and family members. Then test it on people you meet for the first time. Make a mental note of what gets their attention and leads to a longer conversation.

Henry's statement was: 'I'm a banker. I do lots of restructuring.'

Elizabeth said: 'I'm in sales and marketing. I help companies to grow faster.'

Chapter

10

Telling your story

Once someone shows interest in what you do, you will need to tell your story.

Facts tell, stories sell

Most of us find it easier to remember a story than a series of facts. We tell stories about people as a way of illustrating their character or abilities. You can also tell a story about yourself that illustrates your talents, skills and/or experience in an authentic way.

Most finance directors in the UK are accountants in dark suits, aged between 30 and 60. Since every business above a certain size usually has a finance director, there are thousands of people who fit this description. If you asked them whether they were good communicators, practically all of them would say yes. This makes it difficult for a finance director to stand out from the crowd.

On one occasion John interviewed a finance director whose mother tongue is Cantonese. The candidate mentioned that he had attended an awards ceremony in London where he had interpreted for Jackie Chan, the star of many martial-arts films. This anecdote works very well from a branding point of view. In a sentence or two it tells us that (a) he is bilingual/bicultural, (b) he is probably comfortable in front of a large audience and (c) he has connections that extend beyond finance. Above all, it makes him *memorable*.

When you pass on anecdotes about yourself, the facts must stand up to scrutiny. Some headhunters have met several people who claim to have launched the same consumer product or to have completed the same financial transaction. They cannot all be telling the truth. It is more credible to say you were a member of the team that worked on a particular project. You can also be specific about your contribution. Given the scale of the project, the most that anyone can say is that they led the team or were responsible for some particular aspect. The aim is to encourage powerful word-of-mouth advertising rather than expose your-self to ridicule. If you are an upwardly mobile executive, it is better to focus on what your team achieved rather than take all the credit yourself.

Although many people enjoy hearing stories, they still want straight answers to their questions. If someone asks 'Can you do X?', it is best to say yes or no. You can then support your statement with an example. If you avoid giving straight answers, people may feel that you are hiding something.

It usually helps to mention what you are working on right now, particularly if it is a high-profile project. It shows you are in demand. Beware of appearing too busy, however, just in case someone has another project for you.

What to say when you're looking for work

If you have no work right now, it is important to be positive while making it clear that you are looking for a new opportunity. Here are some examples:

- 'I finished at XYZ Co. a month ago. I'm now looking for another full-time role in marketing. In the meantime I'm helping a friend to launch a new product.'

- 'I learned my trade as a financial controller at ABC Hotels. I'm now looking for new opportunities in property and manufacturing.'

- 'I was IT director of FGH until recently. There's a shortage of IT people at the moment, so I've been looking at several really interesting opportunities.'

It is better not to talk about why you left your old company unless the question comes up. In case it does, it is worth preparing a truthful answer that shows you have moved on with a positive attitude. For example:

- 'Last year the overheads doubled just before the revenues halved. Half the staff had to leave, including me, so I'm now looking for another opportunity.'

- 'After the merger, our whole department relocated to Geneva. I couldn't move my family, so I'm now looking for a similar role in this area.'

It is best to keep it brief. The more you talk about the past, the less attractive you will be to new employers, who are interested in what you can do for them *now.* However, at some point you may be asked to summarise your career. You must be clear about who you are and what you want to do. For example:

- 'I've spent most of my career in property, most recently as a business development director for North America. Now I want to *run* a business.'

- 'I've managed businesses in several industries and have led change programmes. Now I'm planning to join a management consultancy firm.'

It is best to be specific, but not prescriptive, about what you are looking for. The person you are talking to may think of someone you should meet and tell you right away. Equally, they may bump into someone a few days later and then get back in touch with you.

Evoking archetypes

By now you have probably chosen one or two archetypes that you are going to evoke consistently. It is equally important not to evoke other archetypes that could dilute your brand. For example, as a business psychologist, David usually evokes the Magician – he helps people to transform their careers. However, he often starts off by evoking the Caregiver, so people feel comfortable and realise they can trust him. If we now refer to some of the other archetypes, we can see how evoking them would be bad for his brand:

- The Explorer: too uncertain. They want solutions, not endless possibilities.

- The Innocent: too ethereal. They want help in dealing with reality.

- The Jester: too flippant. They expect David to take their problem seriously.

- The Lover: inappropriate for a psychologist's relationship with a client!

- The Outlaw: too risky. They do not want a psychologist who breaks the rules.

- The Ruler: too controlling. They want the freedom to find their own way.

Choosing the right metaphor

Spanish philosopher José Ortega y Gasset said: 'The metaphor is perhaps one of man's most fruitful potentialities. Its efficacy verges on magic.' Many of us use metaphors every day. They affect how we think about the world – and behave – in subtle ways. For example, many people say 'time is money'. They talk about 'borrowed time' and 'time running out'. They perceive time as both valuable and limited.

Metaphors can be equally powerful in expressing and strengthening your brand. People often do this unconsciously when they are being authentic. However, metaphors can also work against you and your brand, so it is worth thinking them through. One example is military metaphors, which rest on the notion that 'work is war'. This can be useful when you are talking about launching a marketing campaign or capturing a share of the market. If you were a chief executive talking to shareholders, you might say, 'We will wipe out the competition' or 'Our marketing offensive will capture X per cent of the market'. This can work well if everything else you say and do evokes the Hero. However, it can clash badly with other archetypes such as the Caregiver. Now imagine that you are the chief executive of a chain of private clinics and you promise to wipe out the competition. In this case the Heroic vocabulary clashes with the Caregiver archetype. Metaphors work only if the archetype they evoke is consistent with the brand you are building.

The other danger of metaphors is that they can descend into clichés, particularly in written material. This makes you look unimaginative. We know one consultancy firm whose website exhorted readers to 'Think outside the box!'. Although the firm wanted to tell people it was creative, the way it did so was unoriginal.

Metaphors work best if used sparingly. Once you know your preferred archetype, you can experiment with metaphors that are consistent with it. When talking to an individual or a small group, you can choose a metaphor that will work with them. If you were saving a company from disaster and wished to evoke the Hero, you might tell the staff and shareholders that the company was 'fighting for survival'. This could inspire them to support you. In a more stable situation you might evoke the Ruler. You could say you were 'strengthening the foundations', thereby encouraging people to place their trust in you. If you were evoking the Creator, you could say you were 'building a platform for growth' or 'bringing forth new talent in the business.' That would help to attract people who wanted to be part of something new and exciting.

Exercise M: Metaphors at work

Think about the main archetype you wish to evoke in your work. Which metaphors would reinforce your brand identity? Which would help you to extend your brand?

Henry decided that artistic metaphors worked best for him. This is what he said about the process: 'I work towards a consensus by asking people to imagine a picture of the way they want their organisation to be. Then I ask them which elements are missing from the picture. Just like any artist, I am in charge. I control the information I receive and apply it in layers like an oil painting until it starts to feel right. Often the parts come together and I have something I can almost frame. I usually start with an outline of what I want to achieve and that helps me to identify the parts of the picture I need to spend more time on.'

The Caregiver and Ruler archetypes come across clearly. Although Henry involves people in his painting, he keeps control of it.

Elizabeth loves architecture, so she finds it an easy metaphor to use in her work. In this example she evokes both the Caregiver and the Hero: 'I build relationships the way well-known architects build eye-catching buildings: standing out from the crowd, pushing back the boundaries, taking risks. People remember me because I'm not afraid to speak out for what I believe needs to happen. I build some strong foundations with stakeholders before I present radical ideas. I get existing clients to mention me. I structure what I'm going to say, based firmly on the brief, but I remain true to myself and I'm never afraid to disagree.'

Using words that evoke your archetype

By choosing your words carefully, you can evoke your main archetype and strengthen your brand identity. Here are the 12 archetypes, with words you can use to evoke them.

The Caregiver

Care. Altruism. Helper. Saint. Protect. Comfort. Nurture. Parent. Helper. Supporter. Affection. Empathy. Commitment. Friendly. Concern.

The Creator

Create. Innovate. Self-expression. Non-conformist. Vision. Invent. Inspiration. Daydream. Fantasy. Decoration. Experiment. Unconventional. Beauty. Aesthetic.

The Explorer

Discover. Seek. Wander. Find out. Adventure. Individual. Pioneer. Freedom. Risk. Fearless. Curious. Explore. Experience. Restless.

The Hero

Courage. Prove your worth. Challenge. Competition. Strong. Powerful. Determination. Persevere. Prevail. Rescue. Discipline. Character. Warrior. Turnaround.

The Innocent

Purity. Goodness. Happiness. Simplicity. Paradise. Trusting. Honesty. Idyllic. Childlike. Rebirth. Perfectionist. Stress-reducing. Romantic. Naive. Mystic.

The Jester

Live for the moment. Breaking the rules. Impulsive. Joker. Trickster. Prankster. Clown. Entertainer. Fool. Mischievous. Manipulative. Playful. Lighthearted. Outrageous. Clever.

The Lover

Partner. Intimate. Harmony. Sensory. Pleasure. Intimacy. Beautiful. Romance. Relationship. Attractive. Passion. Erotic. Gratitude. Appreciation. Commitment. Friendship.

The Magician

Realise a vision. Transform. Change. Spiritual. Mediator. Finds win–win solutions. Makes dreams come true. Synchronicity. Meaningful coincidences. Charisma. The experience of flow. Miracles.

The Ordinary Guy/Girl

Connect. Belong. Friend. The boy or girl next door. Good neighbour. Down-to-earth. Humanitarian. Functional. Straightforward. Wholesome. Realist. Team spirit. Unpretentious.

The Outlaw

Break the rules. Revolutionary. Rebel. Disrupt. Destroy. Outrageous. Radical. Counter-culture. Unacceptable. Unconventional. Outsider. Independent thinking.

The Ruler

Boss. Control. Order. Commanding. Authority. Power. Substance. Impressive. Organiser. Responsible. Manager. Administrator. Dominator. Royalty.

The Sage

Scholar. Knowledge. Wisdom. Truth. Objectivity. Expert. Adviser. Mentor. Teacher. Research. Detect. Think. Interpret. Understand.

Storytelling: a powerful way to make a point

Roger E. Jones is a well-known leadership storytelling coach. His latest book is *The Storytelling Pocketbook*. This is what Roger says about using storytelling to convey your message:

'We know anecdotally that stories are memorable, including the stories our friends have told us. Yet few managers and leaders use storytelling to communicate their organisations' values, get their people to embrace change and inspire higher levels of performance.

Robin Dunbar, anthropologist and evolutionary psychologist, estimates that around two-thirds of our conversations are about who is doing what and with whom. In other words: stories. So storytelling is second nature to us all. If we develop our innate ability to tell stories, we can do so clearly, authentically and effectively.

Most people use facts, figures and rational arguments to try and convince others. They rarely succeed. But stories can convey emotions effectively and bring energy to our communication. We remember what we feel. And it's our emotions that inspire us to take action, not facts.

Stories spark our interest and transport us in our imaginations to places where we can visualise the events being recounted.

Stories also help prevent what psychologists call 'confirmation bias' – the tendency to favour information that confirms our preconceptions, regardless of whether that information is true. Confirmation bias causes people to gather evidence and recall information from memory selectively, and then interpret it in a biased way. So if someone tries to convince us to change our minds with facts and figures, we often dig our heels in and resist.

Confirmation bias occurs in change-management initiatives, sales situations and financial decisions, for example. Our personal beliefs are also subject to confirmation bias. However, if you tell a story, it will gently guide the listener to your conclusions, without provoking them with opposing facts. If you think about it, great leaders are also great storytellers.

So bring your communication to life and make it memorable by using a story to make your point. You can then back it up with appropriate facts and figures.'

Further information can be found at www.RogerEdwardJones.com.

Chapter

11

Aligning your CV with your brand

Many people have a standard CV which has acquired bits and pieces over time and become cluttered. It is worth starting again with a blank sheet of paper. Your CV is an important marketing document. People will judge you on the basis of its quality and accuracy.

Make sure your CV conveys your purpose

If you are following a well-trodden path, your CV may speak for itself. A logical progression from one blue-chip employer to another can tell the story well enough.

However, many careers do not follow this pattern. If you have changed role or sector, your CV can start to look messy, particularly if you have done some consultancy work or started your own business.

Many employers and recruitment consultants are looking for someone with a standard background to do a standard job – a square peg for a square hole. If you have an unusual combination of skills and experience, you are unlikely to fit. The odds of success are low if you are competing against candidates who do have the standard background. However, if you package your experience correctly, and evoke your archetype, you can make yourself much more attractive to an employer who wants what you have to offer.

Tailor your CV to your market

You will use your CV in different ways, depending on who you are talking to. We see three main markets for your CV:

1 People who are introducing you.

2 Prospective employers.

3 Recruitment consultants/headhunters.

We will discuss these one by one.

People who are introducing you

Someone may be helping you to find a job, including you in a business plan for a new venture, or inviting you to speak at a conference. Here is a format for a one-page CV which you can use in those situations:

SUNITA SHAH

(www.sunitamshah.com)

Flat 3, 30 Hill Street, London W1 8VY, United Kingdom

PERSONAL DETAILS

Date of birth:	10th October 1983
Nationality:	British and Indian

CAREER TO DATE

2009–Present	**EXTRATERRESTRIAL SOFTWARE, INC**
	(An IT services business with revenues of €90m)
2011–Present	Business Manager, Europe (revenues: €50m)
2009–2011	Business Development Manager, eBusiness
2004–2008	**VEDASOFT, INC**
2006–2008	Business Development Manager
2004–2006	Marketing Executive, New Delhi

EDUCATION

2008–2009	**INSEAD**
	MBA
2001–2004	**THE LONDON SCHOOL OF ECONOMICS**
	BSc Economics (2.1)

LANGUAGES

English:	Mother tongue
Hindi:	Fluent
French:	Fluent
Italian:	Working knowledge

Prospective employers

They often like to see a two-page CV, in reverse chronological order. For example:

Robert Wallis

Robertwallis23@hotmail.com   Mobile + 44 7950 181 858

Growtomorrow PLC
eMarketing Manager – Stayfit   **2010–present**

Growtomorrow is the UK's third-largest food supplements company, with annual revenues in excess of £14m and over 15,000 employees worldwide.

Responsibilities:

To develop and champion Stayfit's global digital strategy, disseminating it worldwide and to senior stakeholders. To provide company-wide thought leadership, engaging and inspiring brand teams, sharing best practice and managing an international team.

Achievements:

- Led business-to-consumer (B2C) loyalty programme, based on insight and attitudinal segmentation, delivering tailored messaging during first 12 months of use, increasing loyalty in 83% of consumers

- Developed digital strategy and launched key commercial sites to support brand positioning and communication campaigns
- Launched a clinical trials alert service, delivering key messages to over 3,000 target customers
- Increased traffic to website by over 200%, to 80,000 visitors in 2011
- Contributed to annual global sales growth of 47% by successfully using Display, PPC and SEO to disseminate key messages
- Undertook competitor, situational and brand strategy analysis to run workshops and develop, agree and prioritise local digital strategy, within the global strategy
- Piloted B2C CRM strategy in two key markets to demonstrate the value of the digital channel alongside the sales force and other channels
- Produced detailed monthly dashboards looking at key metrics and key performance indicators (KPIs) for senior stakeholders

Newbank – Group Account Director   2009–2010

Responsibilities:

To switch the communication strategy from a product to a customer focus, whilst relaunching Newbank's loyalty programme and managing the agency account team.

Achievements:

- Increased warmth to Bank by 25% in key segments. The softer sell was more palatable
- Showcased Bank's expertise in context, highlighting relevance where direct marketing had failed
- Launched new, segmented magazine, increasing selling opportunities
- Introduced robust measurement/evaluation techniques, by channel, to substantiate business claims

Antiarms International UK –
Corporate and Affinity Manager   2007–2009

Achievements:

- New branding, new partners and products for programme, re-launched to members through major B2C campaign
- Welcome pack and lifestyle questionnaire for new members, with response rates of 30%+
- Data-driven promotions across a range of media, with response rates of 10% to 15%
- Revenue increased from £100k to £330k+ per month in 24 months
- Key-note speaker at Money Marketing conference

Betterhealth (B2C health website),
Internet Business Development Manager   2007

- Developed commercial strategy for month-on-month growth of 20% through partnerships and online promotions
- Developed revenue models (market research, advertising, sponsorship) and transactional deals
- Content syndication across various media channels

The Major Illness Research Programme,
Corporate Development Manager   2006

- Most successful affinity card launch: 5,000 cards issued raising over £25k in first 6 months
- CRM promotion with Chocolight, CRC branding and royalty on 2 million containers

Language Solutions Ltd, Sales & Marketing Manager   2005

- Negotiated B2C partnership publicising Language Solutions to over 2.5 million target customers across Europe, at no cost to the company

Education

University of Salford	**2001–05**
Bsc (Hons) 2:1 in Spanish and Economics	

St Mary's College, Norwich	**1994–2001**
9 GCSEs including Maths and English	
3 A-Levels – English, Spanish & Economics	

Personal

Nationality: British   **Languages:** Spanish & French

LinkedIn Profile: *http://www.linkedin.com/robertwallis*

Recruitment consultants/headhunters

They often prefer a one-page summary, followed by 2–3 pages of detail, describing what happened. The first page can be similar to the one-page CV we showed on page 119. This format enables them to get most of their questions answered quickly. It also gives them the information they need to write an appraisal and present you to their clients without too much extra effort.

DAVID BROWN

Date of birth: 30/4/69	Home: +44 121 7000 0000
Married, with two children	Work: +44 121 7111 1111
72 Leicester Road, Birmingham	Mobile: +44 7770 123 123
B3 5NH, UK	david@brown.net

CAREER TO DATE

2006–Present   **THE MID-CAP COMPANY PLC**
(Revenues: £330m)
Group Finance Director

2003–2006   **THE MULTINATIONAL COMPANY, INC**
2004–2006   Finance Director, Cat Food Division (£300m)
2003–2004   Financial Controller, Dog Food Division (£280m)

1994–2003   **THE VERY BIG COMPANY PLC**
1998–2003   Manager, Financial Planning & Analysis
1994–1998   Financial Analyst

1990–1994   **THE BIG ACCOUNTANCY FIRM**
Audit Trainee to Audit Manager

OTHER

2010–Present   Non-Executive Director, Hi-Tech Software Plc

QUALIFICATIONS

1993   **THE INSTITUTE OF CHARTERED ACCOUNTANTS**
First-time passes (Fellow 2003)

1990   **UNIVERSITY OF MANCHESTER**
BSc Economics, 2.1

LANGUAGES   English: mother tongue
French: fluent business level

PROFESSIONAL EXPERIENCE

1990–1994   **THE BIG ACCOUNTANCY FIRM**
1990–1993   Audit Trainee
1993–1994   Audit Manager

I joined The Big Accountancy Firm straight from university, having received offers from several of the 'Big Eight' firms. My audit clients were privately held and mid-cap companies in engineering, insurance, banking and business services.

I passed my professional examinations at the first attempt and was promoted to Audit Manager. My intention had always been to move out of the profession into industry. Within a year I was approached to join The Very Big Company as a Financial Analyst. I accepted their offer.

1994–2003   **THE VERY BIG COMPANY PLC**
1994–1998   Financial Analyst
1998–2003   Manager, Financial Planning & Analysis

The Very Big Company was the global market leader in the production of High-Performance Widgets (HPWs). It had revenues of £900m and a market capitalisation of £1bn. I was based at their Birmingham headquarters, where I reported to the Deputy Group Finance Director.

I worked on many projects, including the following:

- Analysis of manufacturing costs, comparing plants in the UK, France and Taiwan. As a result, a decision was taken to close the French plant and concentrate production in the other two locations.

- Developing a financial model to evaluate a potential investment in a new production line. Using Net Present Value techniques, I concluded that the investment should proceed. The Board accepted my recommendation.

- Etc.

You may find that you need to keep only two CVs updated on your computer: a two-page version and a four-page version. If someone wants a one-page CV, you can send them the one-page summary at the front of the four-page version.

Your CV is one of several tools that people will use to find out more about you. They may also look at websites, your Facebook, Twitter and LinkedIn pages and any videos you have uploaded.

The aim is to get them to meet you

Many people think their CV and covering letter/email will get them the job they want, so they cram in too much information. Unfortunately, this greatly reduces the chances of success. The aim is to get a meeting with the organisation you are writing to, or at least speak to someone on the phone. Your written material should give them just enough information to entice them to find out more about you.

- If your covering letter/email is clear and concise, people are much more likely to read it. If you summarise what you have to offer in a few bullet points, as we described on page 101, the recipient will be able to decide whether to read it themselves or forward it to someone more appropriate in their organisation.

- If the bullet points match some or all of their needs, they are likely to be interested in your CV. If your covering letter/email is too long or badly written, it may languish in an in-tray, until they figure out what to do with it – which often means sending you a 'thanks but no thanks' letter.

- When they look at your CV, it will probably be for 5–20 seconds initially. If they do not immediately see how they or a colleague can use it, it is likely to end up in the 'no' pile.

- If they decide to use it themselves, they will start to spend more time on it. Be prepared for them to call you with no warning. Prepare the answers to questions they are likely to ask you.

- Avoid obvious turn-offs, such as boasting about your abilities or criticising your former employer. Remember that recruiters are used to assessing the content of a CV and look for people who are realistic about their abilities.

- Test the market by showing your covering letter/email and CV to people who have high standards and an eye for detail. Get their feedback on the layout and use of English. Notice anything they find confusing and make it clearer. It is very easy to use jargon, but plain English is far more effective.

- If you have a high-quality blog or website, include the domain name prominently on your CV. That way, they can find out more about you. Videos can be very effective. Once people see you and hear you speak, they begin to feel they know you, even if they have never met you.

- Make it obvious how they should contact you. Provide one phone number and one email address at the top of your CV. (If you provide several of each, it may slow the process down.)

The clearer your communication, the more likely you are to be interviewed for roles that really interest you.

Chapter

12

Your appearance, voice and behaviour

Some of the famous people we mentioned earlier communicated their purpose and their archetype through their appearance and surroundings. You can do the same.

Pierre

Pierre, a business development director, is a good example. He grew up on both sides of the Atlantic and speaks several languages. He is now based in London, where he works for a company that evokes the Ruler. His favourite archetype is the Explorer. It happens to fit his job, which is to explore European markets for opportunities to expand the business.

Most of his colleagues have dark leather briefcases that are consistent with the Ruler. Pierre, however, carries a brown leather shoulder bag with a large flap and a buckle. He also has a small suitcase with wheels, which is handy when he travels by train or by plane. Both are consistent with the Explorer. Pierre chose his luggage before he learned about archetypes. However, he recalls that his new boss commented favourably on his shoulder bag at the interview.

His office is neutral, except for a map of the countries he is currently exploring. At home he has lots of books about Africa and other faraway places. If Pierre keeps some of them in his office it will help him to evoke the Explorer. So could souvenirs from distant continents or a model of the space shuttle. Photos of hot-air balloons gliding over dramatic landscapes would have a similar effect.

Since Pierre's role has been created recently, colleagues sometimes ask what he is *for*. His accessories and surroundings will help to answer that question. They will support his efforts to expand the business into new markets.

Your clothing

In choosing your clothes, it is worth thinking about the archetype you are going to evoke, both within your organisation and externally. Maybe you are the founder of a technology company and have brilliant ideas that others help to implement. If so, you may wish to evoke the Creator, using highly original clothing. You might also choose an unusual hairstyle, as Albert Einstein did. If you are breaking the rules within your industry, you may wish to evoke the Outlaw, deliberately failing to conform to the accepted dress code in your sector.

Although ties are becoming scarcer, they tend to reappear when people are raising money or looking for a job. There are good reasons for this. If you are raising money, formal attire helps to evoke the Ruler. Investors and/or lenders will be more confident that you will keep the business firmly under control and protect their interests.

There is also a cyclical aspect to men's clothing. According to Alan Flusser, the designer and author, men have historically opted for ties during periods of economic uncertainty. Sales of ties usually go up during financial downturns. If you want to keep your job, it is a good time to evoke the Ruler more than you might do otherwise.

Whatever the dress code in your organisation, you can choose to wear clothes that also evoke your archetype. For example, if everyone in your office wears smart casual, you can evoke the Outlaw by including something outrageous in your wardrobe. Or you can evoke the Ruler by wearing an expensive accessory that is in short supply.

Hence investment bankers and hedge-fund managers in casual clothes often wear expensive mechanical watches, despite being surrounded by electronic gadgetry. A Creator in a smart-casual environment could wear something at the forefront of fashion, thus remaining innovative in a conformist environment. It is good to dress stylishly, whether the mode is conservative, casual or flamboyant.

Henry and Elizabeth

Henry's clothing reflects the long period he has spent in banking. He tends to wear a dark grey or blue suit with a pin-striped shirt. These days he usually does not wear a tie in the office, although he always has one ready for an unexpected meeting with a client. He tends not to stand out from his colleagues, preferring to merge into the background by wearing the banking uniform.

Elizabeth's approach is different. Since she works in sales and marketing, it helps to stand out and be memorable. She wears a high-quality scarf and shoes that make her stand out from the crowd. However, she has recently toned down her colours. She now wears a tailored business suit that evokes the Ruler, reflecting her intention to move into senior management.

Exercise N: Observing archetypes in other people and in your surroundings

Next time you are waiting in a reception area, observe your surroundings and the people who work there. Which archetypes do the reception area and other parts of the building evoke? Does the way people are dressed support the same archetype?

If an organisation evokes a particular archetype, it can attract new recruits and help to retain employees. For example, financial institutions often evoke the Ruler and resonate with people who are attracted by that archetype. An organisational development consultancy, meanwhile, might evoke the Caregiver and the Magician, thereby resonating with people who are attracted by those two archetypes.

Your voice

How do you sound to other people? There can be a big difference between what *you* hear and what *they* hear when you speak. They hear sound waves travelling through the air; you hear them partly through your skull. As a result, your voice will probably sound harsher to them than it does to you. It is worth recording your voice on high-quality equipment, so you know how you sound. Then you will at least be aware of how you come across to other people.

Make sure your accent is clear and authentic

A regional or national accent can strengthen your brand if there is a positive association with your work. If you are a French-born chef, keeping your accent can emphasise your association with top-quality food. A Californian accent may help if you work in technology.

Above all, your accent should be *authentic,* unlike some rock musicians whose mid-Atlantic drawl fades minutes into a performance or television interview.

We all grow up speaking with a particular accent. Most of us find it difficult to change it. However, with a bit of effort, we can slightly adjust the way we speak to make our speech clear and attractive to a large audience. A voice coach can help. Here are two examples:

■ Many people in the UK omit to pronounce certain consonants, particularly t's. This makes it hard for listeners to identify words in a sentence unless they know them already. It can be a particular handicap if you are speaking to people whose first language is not English.

▓ Nasal accents are common in North America and certain parts of the UK. They can be both distinctive and attractive. However, some people find a strong nasal accent difficult to listen to for long periods. A nasal accent can be softened with practice.

Your intonation can help to evoke your archetype

Some common habits of speech clash with the speaker's archetype and weaken their brand. One example is *up-speak:* the voice rises at the end of each sentence, making statements sound like questions. If you are a senior executive evoking the Ruler, this will detract from your brand by injecting a note of uncertainty. Likewise, if you normally evoke the Hero, any uncertainty will discourage people from following you.

There are many examples of people using their voices to strengthen their brands and be more effective. Margaret Thatcher worked with a coach from the National Theatre to lower and deepen her voice. It helped her to evoke the Ruler and become Britain's first female prime minister. Winston Churchill evoked the Hero through his intonation and the pace at which he delivered his speeches.

Use gestures to support what you are saying

You may have been taught not to move your hands when you speak. We beg to differ. If you use your hands to support what you are saying, it gives you more energy and enthusiasm. Singers do this in recording studios, even when no one is looking except the producer. Your gestures simply need to support your message rather than distracting people from it.

Your attitude and behaviour

Our behaviour is shaped by the way we see the universe and our place within it. In this section we will describe an approach that is thousands of years old but is new to most people.

Many of us live on the basis of an unspoken assumption: that we are separate from everyone and everything around us. This is known as *duality* – a split into two. Dualistic thinking pervades our lives. We divide the universe into pairs of opposites: them and us, black and white, good and evil, and so on. This habit is so ingrained that we may never think about it. However, all conflict is based on duality. It happens at work, in our social lives and in the strife between religious and ethnic groups.

Duality leads people to see themselves as separate from each other and from the rest of the universe. It is sometimes described as the *illusion of separation*. As Albert Einstein apparently once put it: 'A human being is part of the whole, called by us "universe", a part limited in time and space. He experiences himself, his thoughts and feelings as something separated from the rest – a kind of optical delusion of his consciousness.'

Many people's attempts at marketing themselves are based on dualistic thinking. They try very hard to *get* something – and it shows. It often makes their efforts counterproductive. For example, they pester their contacts in the hope of being rewarded with a job or an assignment. They send the same CV several times to any headhunter or employer they know. Unfortunately this makes them look needy, which is bad news when building any kind of relationship. The underlying message is: 'Please give me a job or project to work on. Otherwise I'll starve.' If you ask them whether they feel comfortable doing all of this, most will say no. Fortunately there is a better way.

All is one

This view goes back thousands of years and is known as *unity*, a central theme of Vedantic philosophy. As it says in the *Chandogya-Upanishad*: 'In the beginning, there was mere being, one without a second.' In other words, everything is part of the whole. The practice of yoga, translated as *union*, belongs to this tradition. As the Brazilian author Paulo Coelho put it in *The Alchemist*: 'All things are one'.

In many ways, *unity* is a convincing description of reality.

In physical terms, we exchange cells with each other, and with our surroundings, all the time. Intellectually, we are more closely linked than we sometimes imagine, since there is clearly a degree of shared consciousness among human beings. One example is when scientists working independently in different parts of the world discover something simultaneously.

In emotional and spiritual terms, we interact with everyone around us. We readily talk about the atmosphere in a room full of people, or the feeling we had about what was going on during a meeting. The social links are obvious. Most of what we do requires the close involvement of other people. For example, it would be virtually impossible to do our jobs, raise children or perform most pieces of music without other people's cooperation. We rely on our environment for many things, from clean air to healthy food, to living without fear of some natural disaster destroying our homes. All human activity has an impact on our environment. It is only a matter of time before we feel the effect of our actions.

In the second half of the twentieth century, physicists began pursuing the idea that everyone and everything is connected. In 1964 Bell's Theorem stated that 'all objects and events in the cosmos are inter-connected with one another and respond to one another's change of state'. David Bohm, one of Albert Einstein's colleagues, took it a step further, describing an 'invisible field that holds all of reality together, a field that possesses the property of knowing what is happening everywhere at once'.

What goes around comes around

Unity has major implications for the way you build your brand. Since you are connected with everyone and everything, whatever you think, say or do will affect everyone, including you. When you serve one person, you are serving everyone, including yourself.

Whatever you do comes back to you in some form. In other words, what goes around comes around. This is one interpretation of the law of karma, also known as the law of cause and effect. (Contrary to popular belief, karma has nothing to do with being calm, it just sounds similar in English.) If you focus on *serving* people rather than trying to get something from them, good things will come back to you sooner or later. This idea is common to many religions and philosophies. In the New Testament, St Paul wrote that 'a man reaps what he sows'. The Dhammapada, in the Buddhist tradition, says that 'if a man speaks or acts with an impure mind, suffering follows him as the wheel of the cart follows the beast that draws the cart … If a man speaks or acts with a pure mind, joy follows him as his own shadow'. According to the Koran, 'if any does good, the reward to him is better than his deed'. Since there is no way of knowing when or how the effect of your actions will come back to you, you do not need anything from the person you are serving right now. Good things are just as likely to come back to you via someone else. For example, this can happen when your reputation for serving people attracts new customers.

A saleswoman might give helpful advice to Mr A, telling him not to buy her product because it will not meet his needs. Then A recommends her to Mr B, who becomes a customer. Equally, if the saleswoman were to mislead Mr A, Mr B would soon find out. She would lose potential customers, starting with B.

Sometimes the delay between giving and receiving is unexpectedly short. During an economic downturn a few years ago, John was invited to give a talk to a large group of business school graduates. The theme was how to get a job via headhunters. Most people in the audience were either unemployed or feared they soon would be. John explained as clearly as he could how they should approach executive search firms. The next speaker, from a large, blue-chip company, explained how he and his colleagues went about hiring people. He also mentioned that he was having trouble filling a senior position. Within a short while he had hired John and his team to solve the problem.

Karma is not only a question of what you *do*. What you *think* and *say* are also important. Your intention towards other people must be positive. Your thoughts, speech and actions will then be aligned. You will also feel good, which will make you more attractive to others, including customers, clients and colleagues. Everyone will benefit, including you.

People sometimes object that the motivation is selfish, since you expect to benefit at some point. However, this objection is itself dualistic – based on the illusion that each of us is separate. Once you see yourself as part of the whole, both giving and receiving become natural and enjoyable. They are effectively the same thing. When you give to others, you are giving to yourself.

The following exercise will help you to see yourself in other people.

Exercise 0: Seeing yourself in other people

Now put yourself in the shoes of people you see or meet. How do they feel? What are they concerned about? What are their hopes? What do you have in common with them?

The more you see yourself in other people, the stronger will be your connection with them. If you keep practising this exercise you may notice some interesting changes. Some people tell us they have noticed other people smiling at them. Then they realise that they have been smiling themselves. The more we connect with other people, the easier and more enjoyable our lives become.

Your attitude affects your behaviour, which is an aspect of your brand. The following exercise will give you a clearer idea of how you behave towards other people and how they perceive you.

Exercise P: Your behaviour

Here is a list of questions about how you behave towards other people. It is not a score-card. Even if it were, no one would score 100 per cent. You may already be excellent in some respects. There may also be areas where you could strengthen your brand quickly by making some improvements.

- How quickly and thoroughly do I return phone calls and reply to emails?

- Am I approachable, or do people have to judge my mood before they talk to me?

- Do I do what I have promised? (If not, it may be better to make fewer promises, giving you time to fulfil those you do make.)

- Do I help people spontaneously? (For example, you might spot a potential opportunity for them and tell them about it.)

- Does my behaviour fit my archetype? (If you evoke the Caregiver, are you caring at all times, or could people conclude that you don't care? If the Ruler is your archetype, do you evoke it consistently, giving people reassurance?)

Henry and Elizabeth

Henry and Elizabeth gave this short questionnaire to people who knew them well. Henry discovered that people found him lax in returning phone calls. Some said he had been quite brusque the first time they had met him. However, once they had got to know him he had become much warmer. He praised people spontaneously and did his best to help them. They identified the Caregiver as his main archetype, followed by the Ruler. They included the Ruler because of the unapproachable, even arrogant, stance he sometimes adopted.

Henry realised he felt uneasy when he met people for the first time. Some of them interpreted this as arrogance. He worked with a coach who made a video of him in action with his team and then helped him to become more open with people, establishing eye contact in a friendly manner. He also developed his listening skills, so he could build a stronger rapport more quickly.

Elizabeth's contacts tended to see the Creator in her rather than the Hero. They noted her determination to be herself and get her own way, convincing those around her that she was right.

She recognised that this perception could hinder her progress in a large organisation. People could see her as more detached than she wished to be.

She realised that she needed to listen more and involve others. This would help her to take on more responsibility.

Once you begin to understand how other people perceive you, it becomes much easier to adapt your behaviour so you can fulfil your potential.

Chapter

13

Charisma

Some people consistently attract colleagues, clients, customers, investors and/or fans. This personal magnetism is often described as *charisma*. It is a valuable aspect of a strong personal brand. However, you cannot fake it. It has to come from within.

We believe there are three main ways in which you can develop more charisma. This chapter will show you how.

Presence

Some people have a strong presence. You can feel it when you are with them. They establish a rapport with you.

What is presence? One aspect is giving people your complete attention – literally being present. You are with them in the here and now – not in the past or the future, or in some other place. Many successful business people, entertainers and politicians are good at being present. If someone is present *with you*, they give their full attention to what you are saying and doing, and what you may be thinking and feeling. Their presence enables them to connect with everyone they meet.

We can also understand presence when we experience a lack of it. Some people are not present when they communicate. The words come out of their mouths, but they are somewhere else. If you watch people during a meeting, you can see that some are not present at all.

We all have distracting thoughts. A person of average intelligence absorbs spoken information six times faster than they speak. If you are highly intelligent, you will have even more time to be distracted. You may find yourself thinking about how you are going to respond. All this gets in the way of communication. It is not enough for you to listen. The other person wants to *feel* listened to. They can tell if you are giving them your full attention. If you do listen and pay attention, you can build a strong rapport with them.

The following exercise will help you to calm your mind and be present.

Exercise Q: Being present

This exercise takes 5–10 minutes. It is important to sit upright during this exercise – if you lie down, you may fall asleep. It is best if someone reads it out while you close your eyes and listen. Alternatively, you can record it and play it back. Whoever reads it out should leave big pauses between each paragraph.

'Sit upright on your chair. Keep your feet flat on the floor and as far apart as your hips. Keep your hands open in front of you and rest them on your thighs. Close your eyes. Allow your body to relax, letting go of any tension.

Feel where you are now: the clothes touching your skin, the weight of your body on the chair, the air on your face and hands.

Become aware of taste and smell. Listen as far as possible into the distance, beyond the sounds nearby.

Listen carefully for a while.

Let go of any mental comments or judgements about the sounds. Rest your attention on the breath as it flows in and out of your body. Do not try to change any of this. Simply allow your attention to rest upon your breath.

Every now and then your attention will wander. When it does, do not judge yourself. Simply bring your attention gently back to the breath.

Open your eyes. Notice the colour and form of the objects around you. Feel the weight of your body on the chair, the air on your face and hands. Remain aware of this for a while.

Most people have to do this exercise several times before it has a major effect. It helps you develop a *quiet mind.* As it says in the Chinese classic *Tao Te Ching:* 'Empty yourself of everything. Let the mind become still.' Although it takes effort, it brings many benefits. One of them is a stronger rapport with other people. The more carefully you listen to them, the more information you will absorb and the better they will feel about you.

Once you have practised this exercise a few times on your own, you can use aspects of it when you are with other people. For example, when you are listening to someone speak, you can feel the breath flowing in and out of your body at the same time. This helps to prevent your attention from wandering off elsewhere. Another example is when you are standing on a stage, speaking to a large audience. Every now and then you can pause and feel the sensations throughout your body, or the weight of your body on the floor. It will help to ensure that you remain present with your audience and are not carried away by what you are saying.

Technology can disrupt your rapport with other people, if you allow it. If you leave your mobile phone switched on, or keep looking at a computer screen, you cannot give someone your full attention. One solution is to take out your mobile and say, 'I'm going to switch this off now'. You then do so and leave it on the table. Many people will follow your example.

Acceptance

Some people's charisma comes from *acceptance.* They accept themselves as they are and the situation as it is. They also accept other people.

You can feel when someone accepts. They are at peace and do not pretend to be anything. They do not judge themselves or other people. They accept you exactly as you are. Sometimes you can sense it in their body language and their smile, and in the way they treat you. Acceptance is an aspect of love – it draws people to you.

If you accept things as they are, rather than as you think they should be, then you can make appropriate plans and take action. As Deepak Chopra says: 'Accept the present, intend the future.'

Here is an exercise to help you accept.

Exercise R: Acceptance

Before you get out of bed, say to yourself: 'Today I shall accept everything that occurs.' As you go about your daily activities, keep returning to the present moment. This will help you to observe what is going on around you. Notice the way people speak and behave, the weather, the pace at which things happen or don't happen. Notice the thoughts that appear in your mind. Say to yourself: 'I accept everything that occurs.'

If you remain in the present you can also observe any judgements as they appear in your mind: 'She shouldn't have said that', 'People shouldn't do that', 'What a stupid situation' and so on. However, instead of clinging to these judgements, you can let them go. Don't try to resist them. You can just let them go.

Imagine you are standing on a bridge, looking down into a river as it rushes past. All kinds of thoughts, including judgements, are carried along down the river, while you observe them. Fairly soon they will vanish. New ones may appear. You can let go of them, too. Say to yourself: 'I accept everything that occurs.'

You still *care* about what goes on around you. If you remain in the present, you can take the right action at the right time. If a child or a dog runs out into the road, you can intervene immediately. However, whether observing or taking action, you avoid judging. It frees you from negative emotions that sap your energy. It helps you do what needs to be done, at just the right time.

Once you have taken the necessary action, you can relax. Place your attention on the breath flowing in and out, and on the sensations throughout your body. Return to the present moment. Say to yourself, 'I accept everything that occurs.'

Presence is not easy to pin down. However, we know it when we see it or feel it in someone else. If you (i) remain in the present and (ii) accept yourself and others, you will develop a stronger presence of your own.

Pursuing your mission/purpose

We talked about your mission in Chapter 6. It involves applying the talents you love to use, in a way that is consistent with your values, to an activity that absorbs you. If you pursue your mission, people are likely to be attracted by the energy you exude when you do what you love. Some will be attracted by your talent(s), particularly if they have a similar talent but have not fully applied it yet. For example, some people have a talent for leadership, but have yet to realise it.

Tribes is a thought-provoking book written by marketing guru Seth Godin, who says: 'Leadership ... is about creating change that you believe in. ... Through your actions as a leader, you attract a tribe that wants to follow you. The tribe has a worldview that matches the message you're sending ... I think most people have it upside down. Being charismatic doesn't make you a leader. Being a leader makes you charismatic.'

Above all, be authentic

As we said in chapter one, if you are true to your talents and your values, you will be *authentic*. While some people will keep their distance from you, you will also attract people who share some of your values and appreciate what you do best. It is much easier to work with people who are on the same wavelength. It is also far more productive and enjoyable.

Chapter

Getting paid

It is time to talk about money. Some people are squeamish about this. Either they accept whatever money they are offered or they ask for very little, for fear of being too expensive. Others are completely unrealistic and ask for more than the job is worth. Once you understand the market value of what you are doing, you can either accept it or find a way of adding more value that people are prepared to pay for. Sometimes it only takes a change of approach – or a change of customer – to earn a lot more from essentially the same activity.

Pricing is an important aspect of your brand

Not only does the price you charge affect your material wellbeing in the short term, it also has a long-term effect on how people perceive you, whether they want to work with you, whether they recommend you, and so on. It is therefore worth thinking carefully about the price you charge.

The context is important here. In some situations it is necessary to research the market and negotiate your remuneration. In other situations there is less need to do so.

- If you are an intern or a trainee in a well-regarded company, there may be little sense in trying to negotiate your salary. If you build a reputation for excellent work, your market value will increase and the company will pay more just to keep you. You can still check how much you are worth by talking to recruitment consultants or other people in your industry.

- Once you reach board level, the ability to transfer from one sector to another tends to increase, so you are likely to be paid the market rate. This is particularly true of chief executives, finance directors, chairmen and non-executive directors. In some countries, if a company is quoted on a stock exchange, a remuneration committee decides how much directors are paid and the details are published in the annual report.

- Salaries tend to be most out-of-line with the market somewhere in the middle of large organisations. If you have been with your employer for years, your remuneration may lag behind what people with similar skills are earning elsewhere. The internal pay scale may also hold you back, even if it bears no relation to the market. Some pay scales have no economic rationale. We know a bank where everyone's salary is partly determined by how many people they manage. This means that senior executives in specialist roles cannot earn what they are worth. Some employers subscribe to salary surveys produced by consultancies, which tell them how much they should pay someone for a particular job. However, even surveys cannot provide a definitive answer, since the sector and location have a big influence. The market rate for the job you do will be affected by many factors not captured in surveys.

- If you are self-employed it is even more important to check market rates, so you know roughly what you could be charging. Whether you receive that amount depends partly on the value clients place on your services. If they believe you add a lot of value, they will pay your fees and recommend you to others. If you are building a top-quality brand, you should probably charge a premium price, i.e. more than the average supplier of your type of service.

Everyone you are considering working for has a problem that you may be able to solve. It will be causing them some form of pain, ranging from mild to acute. Here are some examples:

- Someone may employ you because, if they do not, they will miss some opportunity to win new business and make a profit.

- Someone may hire you as a consultant because they have a problem they cannot solve on their own. It may be costing them money, causing them discomfort or embarrassment, or just slowing their progress.

■ People may buy your novel or watch your film because they are bored and want to be entertained.

■ Someone may hire you to prevent a disaster from occurring.

If what you do takes away an acute pain for someone, you become a 'must-have' for them. If what you do takes away only a minor pain, you are a 'nice-to-have'. You can charge a lot more for a 'must-have' than you can for a 'nice-to-have'. Another way of looking at it is that you add a lot more value when you provide a must-have product or service.

The question is, how will this added value be divided up? How much will they keep for themselves? How much will they pay you for providing it? In order to capture some of the value for yourself and/or your business, you need to:

Analyse the situation before you negotiate the price

Whether you are employed or self-employed, you will need to negotiate your remuneration at some point. One of the key concepts is the Best Alternative to a Negotiated Agreement, otherwise known as the BATNA.

It is discussed at length in *Getting to Yes* (see Recommended reading on page 235). Both you and the person who wants to hire you have a BATNA. Their BATNA is what they would have to pay someone else to do the same work to the same standard. Your BATNA is the amount you could earn with another employer or client. The Zone of Possible Agreement (ZOPA) is the gap between the two, as shown in the diagram opposite.

Assuming both of you are economically rational, any agreement you reach will be in the ZOPA. If you ask for more than their BATNA, they will be better off hiring someone else. If they offer you less than your BATNA, you will be better off working for someone else.

How do you find out their BATNA? One way is to ask them what the other potential solutions are and make an estimate of what they would cost. Maybe they *could* get someone else to do the work. If there are plenty of other people who could do it, you can find out the going rate. If there are only one or two others, you may be able to find out who they are and what they charge. If there is a recruitment consultant involved, you can ask them how much such people are likely to be paid. As you build your brand, more people will bid for your services. Your BATNA will rise, narrowing the ZOPA in any negotiations. Your earnings are likely to rise, too. (We hope you will agree that this book has been an excellent investment.)

Not only does the strength of your brand affect the price you can charge, it also works the other way round. The price you charge affects your brand. You could set your price low, in the hope of attracting employers or clients. Ironically, this may put them off. If your price is low, it suggests your BATNA is also low. In other words, no one else is prepared to pay much for your services. Potential customers may infer that you are not very good at what you do.

Since a low asking price can damage your brand, it is much better to work out how much value you can add, and then charge a price that captures some of that value. If you are being interviewed by a headhunter, a high salary and bonus can actually work in your favour. Many candidates assume that, if they are highly paid, they are less likely to be interviewed. In fact, the opposite may be true. As with luxury goods, many headhunters find highly priced candidates reassuringly expensive. If someone is prepared to pay you that much, you must be good. If you are far cheaper than they would expect, they may start to wonder whether there is something wrong with you.

We are not suggesting you lie about your remuneration. However, it is good to demonstrate that you know your value in the market. Here are some examples from the distant country of Batnastan, whose currency is the Bat (B):

- 'My current base salary is B100. It's low because I'm working for a start-up. The founders have also given me 5 per cent of the shares. I've recently been considering opportunities with a base salary of around B200, and a bonus of 30–50 per cent.'

- 'I've just come back from an overseas posting where my base salary was B400. However, some of that was danger money – most people don't want to live and work there. The packages I've been considering in Batnastan are in the range of B200 to B300.'

- 'My current base salary is B100. However, I'm flexible about the salary in my next job, provided I do well on my shares if the business succeeds.'

If you have done your homework, you will know your BATNA and have some idea of your employer's or client's BATNA. You can now reach an agreement somewhere in the ZOPA. Where you end up is largely a question of tactics. Imagine you are negotiating your salary with a new employer. You have been interviewed by several other companies and know that you could earn B200 with one of them. You have also done your homework and believe that this particular employer would pay up to B300 for your combination of skills and experience. You believe that if you asked them for more than B300, they would be better off transferring someone from another country to do your job. Alternatively, they could divide your role in two and pay two people B150 each. To sum up, your BATNA is B200 and theirs is B300, as shown in the diagram.

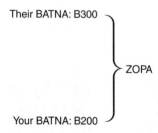

Their BATNA: B300

ZOPA

Your BATNA: B200

In theory you could end up anywhere in the ZOPA between B200 and B300. If you ask for B300 and they offer B200, you will probably end up somewhere in the middle. Splitting the difference at B250 could satisfy both parties. However, if you move quickly and ask for B300 in writing, this could exert a powerful influence on the final outcome. Studies show that agreement is usually reached close to the first price that is mentioned and written down. One possible reason is that the person who makes the first move has done their homework more thoroughly than the other party. If you know exactly what your potential employer wants you to do, and how else they could get it done, you will know their BATNA. Most employers would find it more difficult to work out your BATNA. They could ask you your current salary, but you might be underpaid. In that case your BATNA is the highest salary you could earn elsewhere. However, they may not have the time or inclination to investigate all of this. If asked, you can tell your prospective employer what other companies are likely to offer you.

During salary negotiations with a new company, their pay structure may work in your favour. If they have a standard rate for someone in your role, they may offer it to you without any negotiation. If it is significantly higher than your current salary, you may just accept it.

While these discussions are going on, it helps to keep things in perspective. The best remuneration package is one that works for you and your employer. If you do an even better job than they had anticipated, they may increase your pay in order to keep you.

Chapter

15

Becoming more visible

Once you know who you are and where you are going, it is time to become more visible. There are simple things you can do right away. Later on we will talk about more ambitious ways of putting yourself on the map. This chapter deals with conventional, 'offline' marketing. Chapter 17 is about online marketing.

Business cards

Both authors of this book have attended conferences, even networking events, where people turned up with no business cards. Some of them say: 'Give me your card and I'll email you my contact details'. Very few do so.

It is easy to stand out in this environment. All you need is a clear business card which gives your full contact details, including your phone numbers and your email address. It should also remind people of who you are and what you do.

Most business cards are impersonal, with just a name, a title and a company. However, even these will give people a clue about who you are. It is useful to keep the back of the card blank so you can write a message to remind people of the topic you discussed, or what each of you is going to do to follow up. You can also write the address of your personal website or your page on a social networking site if it is not already on the front of the card.

Speaking to groups

One of the best ways to reach more people is to speak to them in groups. It could be two or three colleagues or clients, it might be ten people around a table, or hundreds at a large venue. Whenever you stand up and say something useful to a large audience, good things tend to happen. Someone might want to discuss a job or consulting project with you, or invite you to speak at another venue. Being a speaker gives you credibility on which you can build.

You may be afraid of public speaking. Many people are terrified. They worry about what the audience will think or say about them. Some people in the audience are also afraid – afraid that you will talk for hours, make weak jokes or endlessly promote your business.

You can overcome this, firstly by changing what you focus on. Unless you are a professional entertainer, you have probably been invited to speak because you know something that could help the audience. All you have to do is *focus* on helping them. If you focus on one thing, it shifts your attention away from everything else, including any unhelpful thoughts. Instead of being self-conscious, you will literally forget yourself. Once people realise you are making a sincere effort to help them, they usually relax and pay attention. Even if you are talking about your own experiences, you can focus on how these will help your audience. Most of them will want to learn from your talk, rather than dismiss it as an ego trip.

Beyond this, public speaking is a question of preparation and practice. The more thoroughly you prepare and the more often you speak, the better you will become.

Getting to know your audience

You may already know your audience well. If not, there are ways to break down barriers and build rapport. One is to find out about them before you speak. Talk to the organiser a few days beforehand. Ask about the audience members' backgrounds, what they want from your talk, what they like and do not like. Their nationalities and cultural backgrounds are also important. If you are going to speak to them in a language other than their mother tongue, think of ways to make it easier for them.

If you arrive at the venue early, you can chat with members of the audience. Those who get there first are usually keen to hear what you have to say. If you talk to them and find out their names, you will already have a few supporters when you stand up and speak.

They are likely to ask good questions and contribute to the discussion at the end of your talk.

Moving around also helps you connect with your audience. Some speakers appear rooted to the spot, twisting their necks so they can read words off the screen behind them. It is better to walk out from behind the desk or lectern and engage with your audience, looking at the screen now and then. If you are talking to a small group, or have a radio microphone, you can walk among them, which is even better. Some talk show hosts do this to great effect.

Addressing one person at a time

If you are speaking to a large audience you may find yourself staring into space, particularly if you are dazzled by floodlights and your eyes have not adjusted. It helps to focus on one sympathetic person at a time and talk to them. To begin with, you may have to focus on someone you can barely see. They and the people around them will usually pay more attention, because they will feel involved. Once you have spoken to them for a few seconds, pick another person in a different part of the room. That way, different groups will be drawn in. Make sure you include someone in the back row and someone on either side of you, so everyone feels involved.

Some television presenters use a simple technique. Although millions of people may be watching, they think of one friend or family member. Then they look into the lens and talk to that person. It helps the presenter to remain relaxed and confident.

Structuring your material coherently

Your talk will be much easier to deliver if you structure it carefully. Then you can relax, put your message across and answer questions. Listeners will grasp your argument and remember more of what you have said. You can do all of this using the *pyramid principle* developed by Barbara Minto. At the top of the pyramid, your presentation should convey the main message. For example, 'Building your brand will transform your career'. This message can be broken down into a series of statements, the first of which is 'You already have a brand'. This becomes the heading on the first slide. You can then break down this statement into a series of points – usually between two and four. If you use PowerPoint, it will help you to apply the pyramid principle. When we give talks on *Brand You*, our first slide often looks like the one shown here.

You already have a brand

- 'Your brand is what people say about you when you are not in the room.' – Jeff Bezos, Founder of Amazon

- It's not just who you know, it's who knows you.

- Most people do not manage their brands. You can.

Some people memorise a speech to accompany their slides. This is a daunting task and usually makes them sound wooden. Equally, you should avoid reading the text word for word, which is boring and causes 'death by PowerPoint'. It is better to use the slides as prompts, so you talk about one point at a time. You can add examples and anecdotes as they occur to you. If you have met some members of your audience, you can include examples that are relevant to them. You will then speak naturally, as you would during a conversation. If possible, allow people to ask brief questions as you go along. They will pay closer attention and learn more. If you relax and enjoy it, your audience will feel good about you and your message.

Humour breaks down barriers and keeps people interested. Some speakers tell set-piece jokes, but that has its risks. People may have heard the joke before. They may not share your sense of humour, particularly if they are from a different culture. For us it feels more natural to make light-hearted remarks as we go along. It is certainly less risky. In some countries such as Britain there is a tradition of self-deprecating humour – making remarks at your own expense. Elsewhere this is not common practice. However, you can still have fun. Your audience would prefer to be entertained as well as informed.

An ideal format is a presentation consisting of ten slides, each of which communicates one point, supported by a series of sub-points. If you allow 2–3 minutes per slide, ten pages of PowerPoint will give you a presentation lasting 20–30 minutes, just the length of time many people can concentrate without a break. They will be grateful if you keep it brief. That also leaves plenty of time for questions and/or exercises.

Once you have given your talk, it is good to post your PowerPoint slides on your host's website. That way, people who were unable to attend can still get the gist of what you said. You can also put your presentation on a website such as SlideShare (www.slide-share.net), and promote it via Twitter, Facebook, LinkedIn, etc.

Some hosts like to record talks by visiting speakers, which you can then promote in a similar way. However, if you are using material from a book or course you have written, be careful about copyright. It can be difficult to package and sell audio material if you have already provided something similar for free.

Once you get used to it, public speaking is no big deal. It is just another way to send your message out into the world. If it is something you really believe in – and you focus on serving your audience – then you will be authentic and find it much easier to overcome any fear of presenting. Your main archetype will come across, through both your material and the way you deliver it. For example, if you are a safety expert giving a talk on how to avoid accidents at work, you may evoke the Caregiver. If you are a stand-up comedian telling people about embarrassing moments in your life, you may evoke the Jester and/or the Ordinary Guy. If you are naturally outrageous, you may evoke the Outlaw.

Television and radio

The audiences for both these media have become highly fragmented. Before spending time on a television or radio appearance it is worth checking how many people tune in and what their backgrounds are. If you are being interviewed, it is essential to be well informed and confident. You should also check why you are being interviewed. Be careful about what you say, as you are likely to be quoted out of context. On one occasion David was contacted by a national television station that wanted him to talk about the effects of an industrial dispute. Three hours later, a presenter and cameraman came to his house and interviewed him for an hour. The following day the news broke and David's interview was reduced to a 15-second sound bite taken completely out of context.

Being quoted in newspapers and magazines

One of the quickest ways to become visible is to be quoted in the press. Articles (and photos) can remain visible on the Web for years. If you become an expert in your field, journalists will approach you at some point. It is a good idea to follow them on Twitter, so you can stay connected with them.

They may be interested in further material. If you are a reliable and accurate source, some will keep coming back. Journalists work to tight deadlines, so they rely on key contacts for an opinion or a quotation that helps to build their story. Many local newspapers and specialist magazines have a small staff and are short of interesting copy. You may find that they publish your article or press release verbatim. However, if you attempt to force-feed a story to journalists, particularly those in the national press, it can backfire. It is much better to treat them with respect and build a reputation as a reliable source of information.

It is best to avoid giving opinions on other people or contentious situations. Quite apart from the legal risks, negative remarks reflect badly on you, the commentator. If an article says you 'declined to comment', it still helps to build your brand. The fact that you were mentioned shows you are an authority. Declining to comment helps to build your reputation for discretion and professionalism.

Writing a letter, article or book

If you enjoy writing and are good at it, an article for a newspaper or magazine can help to build your profile. Writing a letter to the editor is even easier, especially if you do so by email. It is best to say something constructive that other readers will find interesting, rather than simply attacking another person's point of view. If you read previous letters to the editor you will see the kind of material that gets published, and can tailor yours accordingly.

Writing a book requires a lot of effort, but can work wonders for your brand. To begin with, it will strengthen your existing relationships. If anyone has read your book they are likely to think of you next time they have a need. Books can also have a big impact on people you have never met. Most people keep books longer than other material and/or pass them on to friends and colleagues. If your book is published commercially by a third party, it helps to confirm that you are an expert.

Writing a high-quality book that will be read by lots of people takes time and effort. You can conserve energy by finding out what publishers want and writing a synopsis and sample chapter first, in the format they require. One way to do this is to work with an agent, who will help to shape and sell your book in return for a percentage of any advance and/or royalties. However, finding an agent who is willing to represent a first-time author is not always easy. It may be better to start by attending a class or workshop for new authors run by your local writers' club. Examples include

The London Writers' Club (www.londonwritersclub.com) and The California Writers Club (www.calwriters.org). These events will enable you to meet other writers, both published and aspiring, as well as agents, publishers and publicists.

If you are writing purely for existing and potential clients, you may decide to self-publish initially. This is simple and inexpensive. You can either use a print-on-demand service, such as Lulu (www.lulu.com), or approach a book designer and a digital printer directly. Either way, you can produce a few hundred copies, which you either sell or give away. It is also worth using a professional editor to make sure the final version is clear, logical and grammatically correct. Then your book will help you to win more business.

An even cheaper option is to publish your book as an ebook initially, in a format suitable for the Kindle and/or the iPad. The costs of doing so are falling steadily.

If you are an expert in your field, you may wish to write a 'how to' book. If so, it is best to address a specific problem. This will help to make it a must-have for your readers, rather than a nice-to-have. A good example is *Getting to Yes,* the classic text on negotiation that has sold more than 2 million copies in 20 languages.

It is worth visiting a large bookshop to get an idea of what has already been written on the subject. The shop assistant may know of any bestsellers. You can also ask potential readers if they have read anything similar. Did they like it? Would they recommend it to a friend? Once you find a book on the subject you have in mind, look carefully at the style of writing and any case studies that are included.

Amazon is a convenient means of checking whether a title you have in mind has been used by someone else. If so, you can gauge the existing book's popularity by its sales ranking. In some cases it does not matter if you use the same title, particularly if you have a different subtitle, or if the other book is not selling well.

Some books are written only for the UK or the US market. You can increase your sales by adopting an international approach. One example is *The Tao of Coaching* by Max Landsberg, a former partner with McKinsey and with Heidrick & Struggles. His book has sold over 150,000 copies in 20 languages. It is a good idea to write for a global readership and test your manuscript on some non-native speakers of the language in which you are writing. The clearer your text, the easier it will be to translate.

You can still sell a lot of copies in one market, if your book meets a pressing need. A former colleague of ours, Semi Cho, wrote *Global Talent – How to Overcome Cultural Barriers and Become a Globally Competitive Professional*, in Korean. The population of South Korea is 58 million – a little less than France or the UK. Nevertheless, her book appeals strongly to many Koreans' desire to work in international corporations, or see their children do so. It sold 60,000 copies in its first six months and became a top-ten bestseller. Despite living thousands of miles away, Semi has become well known in South Korea and now speaks at conferences throughout Asia.

You may spot a gap in the market while you are looking for a book to recommend to other people. John has done this with two books. David was consistently told by his clients that he should write a book to help young people understand their passions so they could choose the right career.

Once you see an opportunity, you can estimate how big it is. How many people are potential purchasers and how badly do they need the book? Then you can choose a title that will appeal to them. You may change the title between now and publication, but having a working title gives you a sense of direction.

Publishers want to know about the competition your book will face. However, it may actually help you if other writers have established a readership for your subject. If you have something new to say, people will buy your book, too. You can get an idea of how well other books are selling by looking on amazon.com and amazon.co.uk. There are also Amazon websites for the Canadian, Chinese, French, German, Italian, Spanish and Japanese markets. The rankings are updated hourly.

Publishers look for credible authors. They want manuscripts that are *authentic* – written by people who know their subject first-hand and are experts in their field. There is much to be said for writing with a co-author. If you have similar values and expectations, you can produce a much better book than either of you would on your own. There will also be two of you to promote it once it is published. Our experience with *Brand You* is that $2 + 2 = 8$ (at least).

It is easy to write a turgid book on a subject you know well. It is harder, but a lot more fun, to write a book that brings your subject alive and makes it accessible to a wide readership. A good technique is to imagine you are going to read it aloud, with no visual aids. Listeners will want to understand it straight away, with no footnotes or further explanation. Otherwise they will switch off. This approach also makes it easier to turn your manuscript into an audio book – tapping into another large and growing market.

If you base your book on material you have used to teach people, you will already know what they find most useful, most difficult and so on. You will still need to experiment to ensure that readers enjoy the final version and recommend it to others. We do this by giving drafts to friends from different backgrounds and of various nationalities. The book evolves from one draft to the next.

If you are already well known, an autobiography or a book based on your experience and opinions can work extremely well. The bestseller lists in some countries contain lots of them. Politicians, generals, sportspeople and broadcasters have all written best-sellers in this genre – or have had them written for them. They have strong personal brands already, so publishers and readers flock to them. Even convicted criminals have succeeded.

Your book does not have to be about you at all. It could be about a relative, as in the case of *Ken Purkiss – 50 Photos*. Although John and his friends produced it to raise money for charity, it proved unexpectedly popular among his business contacts. Since photography involves capturing the moment, often in unexpected ways, it fits well with the Magician, John's preferred archetype. Books such as this can strengthen your brand by illustrating your heritage in the way we described in Chapter 8. It is rather like the Jack Daniel's adverts that talk about the company's founder and its tradition of whiskey-making in Lynchburg, Tennessee.

History and biography work well for politicians: Winston Churchill is known for his four-volume *History of the English-Speaking Peoples*; William Hague has written books on Pitt the Younger and William Wilberforce. Writing about your forebears emphasises your heritage and strengthens your brand.

Chapter

16

Building your network

Human beings have always had networks of relationships and contacts. However, these days many people's networks change and grow faster than before, due to frequent job moves, geographical mobility and the internet. If you want to manage and build your brand, you have to manage and build your network. But how?

There are plenty of books and seminars on the subject of networking techniques. Yet many of us still feel uncomfortable about cultivating someone in the hope of getting something from them. This negative feeling is a poor way to start a relationship.

The importance of authenticity

Fortunately, there is a simple way to overcome this. The idea that you need to get something from someone is based on the assumption that you are separate from them. This assumption is questionable. It is much better to proceed on the basis that 'all is one'. In other words, you are intimately connected with everyone and everything.

The first few exercises in this book will help you. Once you begin to discover the talents you love to use (Exercises A and B), you will already have a clue to how you can serve other people in a way that benefits everyone. Understanding your values (Exercise C) will show you how you love to use your talents and help to attract people with whom you have values in common. In other words, you and they will be on the same wavelength.

The feeling that we need to get something from someone is usually based on fear – fear that we are not good enough or that we are not valued. This fear often arises because we are living in a way that is not based on who we are; we are trying to be something we are not. The exercises so far are designed to help you be authentic. When we are authentic we are more confident in ourselves and what we can do for others. Once we focus on doing what we love, for and with people who resonate with us, everything changes. It feels much better and is far more effective.

Attracting a powerful network

Our friend Srikumar Rao has a useful technique for putting this into practice. It goes as follows:

- Stop trying to cultivate relationships with people you meet in the hope that they could be helpful to you.

- Next time you meet or hear about someone who is doing something that resonates with you, stop for a moment. It must be something that moves you. For example, they could be making television documentaries, turning around an ailing business or running a charity that helps violent offenders to lead a normal life. It is highly likely that you and that person have values in common.

- Send them a note or email explaining what excites you about what they do. Offer to help them in some specific way. Be prepared to go ahead if they accept your offer.

- Your intention is the key. You are not doing this because you want to form a relationship with them, it is because you believe in what they are doing.

- You will be surprised at how often your offer is accepted. As you fulfil your promise, a powerful network will form around you, without your even having to try.

Opportunities for connecting

Prudence is still essential. We are not suggesting you put personal information online or meet strangers in dark places. However, it is important to be open with people if you want to find a new job or connect with others to develop talents, skills, ideas and businesses. As the saying goes, every opportunity begins with a relationship. The internet, and social media in particular, has helped to make this easier than ever before.

Using technology to manage your network

Many of us have hundreds or even thousands of contacts on social networking sites. Some we know personally and some we do not. You can use contact-management software on your computer and/or your smartphone to keep track of those you know personally. This has the advantage that you can send a message to all of them at once when you need to, for example, when you change jobs. Your IT department or an IT consultant can show you how to synchronise the information in your smartphone with that held in your computer. Your mobile network provider may also be able to help.

17

Building your brand online

Your online presence extends from email to websites, blogs and other social media. We are very grateful to social media expert Jorgen Sundberg (www.linkhumans.com) for his help with this chapter. It is best to approach this subject one step at a time.

Email

It helps if your email address begins with your first name. That way, if people have not contacted you for a while, they may find your email address right away when they type your first name into a blank email. Use a nickname in your email address only if you also use it at work.

Some people's email addresses begin with an initial, their spouse's name, the name of their cottage in the countryside or some unfathomable combination of numbers and letters. Any of these could lose you a potential client or employer. They may spend time trawling through their 'deleted' folder, searching for an old message from you. More likely, they will give up looking.

If you have a common surname, you can use your email address to remind people of who you are and what you do. For example: JoeBloggsWriter@yahoo.co.uk

Sending emails

Email is a good way to stay in touch and is less intrusive than phone calls. If your message has avoided the spam folder and is sitting in someone's inbox, they can read it whenever they want. However, many of us receive emails that we delete unread. People are more likely to read yours if you personalise them. It helps if your email address contains your full name. If not then you can include it in the subject box; for example: *Update from Sally Jones.*

There are some useful online services for managing your email lists, such as Your Mailing List Provider (www.ymlp.com) and

Mailchimp (www.mailchimp.com). They enable you to mail-merge emails to your contacts. You can then send Fred an email that begins 'Dear Fred' rather than 'Dear All' or 'Hi'. Fred is much more likely to pay attention.

Your Web presence

Many people's Web presence consists of a random series of mentions on various websites. The information is often out-of-date and/or inaccurate. The first step, therefore, is to check your presence on the Web.

Exercise S: Conduct an online brand audit

1 Borrow someone else's computer, i.e. one that has no settings specific to you.

2 Type your full name, in inverted commas (e.g.'Jo Smith'), into a search engine such as Google. See what comes up on the first page.

3 Add your name in inverted commas to Google Alerts.Go to www.google.com. Click on 'More', then 'Even more', then 'Alerts'. Then follow the instructions to receive alerts when new material about you (or someone with the same name as you) is published on the Web.

If the first page of results in (2) above leads to a website with your email address or phone number, that is an excellent start.

Now look at what has been written about you, and the context. Is this the brand image you wish to project? Will employers and clients be attracted by what they read?

It is hard to be visible if your name is a common one, such as Janet Jones or Raj Patel. One solution is to make sure you are mentioned in the context of what you do. If your name is John Smith and you are an architect, will people find you if they type 'John Smith' and 'architect' into Google? There may be nothing about you, but plenty about a namesake who is a notorious criminal. If you do not like what you find written about you on the Web, you have three main options:

1 Sue people. We do not recommend this unless what they have written is clearly libellous. Getting into a fight will generate further negative publicity.

2 Become active online, generating positive, constructive comment about you that pushes the old, negative material further and further down the rankings. One of the best ways to do this is to start a blog in your own name and update it regularly. Unless you have a very common name, your blog will soon appear at or near the top of the Google ranking.

3 Hire an online reputation management service to do (2) above for you. There are many such organisations that are easy to find on the Web.

Building your brand online

Before immersing yourself in the details of online marketing, it is best to be clear about what you wish to achieve. The archetypes can help you do this.

Exercise T: Your personal brand strategy

Bring together the results of the exercises you have completed in this book.

Ask yourself the following questions:

1 What are my talents and values?

2 What is my unique combination?

3 Which archetypes do I evoke?

4 Who are the people I want to reach?

5 What do people want from me once they know I exist?

6 In view of my preferred archetype, which metaphors could I use to strengthen my brand online?

Social networks allow you to evoke your archetype on a massive scale. For example, until now you may have evoked the Jester one to one or in small groups. Now you can reach a much larger audience using Twitter or Facebook.

There is a lot of humour on social networking sites, just as there is in many homes and offices. If you are going to be humorous, it is best to do so in a way that comes naturally to you. It should be authentic and fit your personality. Some people naturally make off-the-cuff remarks. You can also forward other people's material, including jokes and videos. It is important to consider which archetypes you are evoking when you do this. Dirty jokes will take you rapidly into Outlaw territory. Do you really want to do that in front of hundreds or thousands of people? Another option is to adopt a naïve approach to humour. That will take you closer to the Innocent.

Setting up a personal website

If you are self-employed, you probably want people to find and contact you. Potential clients may expect you to have a website and assume you are no good if you do not. If you have both a personal and a business website, make sure their messages are consistent, with a similar look and feel.

If you are a media star, a website will help your fans to follow your progress without getting too close. You can also use it to sell CDs, downloads, books or merchandise.

Not everyone wants a website. Some angel investors prefer to keep a low profile. It helps them to avoid being mobbed by entrepreneurs seeking finance. Some salaried employees shudder at the thought of setting up a website. They fear it will smack of self-promotion and send the wrong message to their boss. However, it does not have to be that way. For example, an increasing number of people write blogs about their area of expertise in a way that helps to attract and retain customers for their employers. These blogs can be either on the company's website or on a personal website.

Another solution is to appear on a website for a trade association, an industry body or a charity. If you are a non-executive director, you will have another opportunity to raise your profile on the Web. Researchers in executive search firms look carefully at board members' profiles. As ever, you will be judged by the company you keep.

A personal website can be particularly useful if you are between jobs, i.e. unemployed. It will help you to continue commenting on your chosen field and interacting with people who are involved in it. It will make you more visible to potential employers, business partners and so on.

We believe that personal websites will become more and more widespread, as a complement to your CV. A personal website enables you to bring all your online activities together in one place, as John has done at www.johnpurkiss.com and David has at www.davidroystonlee.com. You only have to give people one web address, i.e. yours, for them to find you on Twitter, Facebook and LinkedIn. They will also find your blog, photographs, audio recordings, video clips, etc. From there you can direct them to other websites relating to your employer, any publications you may have written, other organisations you are involved with and so on. It is best to include your first name and surname in the domain name, so your website is easy to find via Google and other search engines.

You can use your website to communicate your unique combination of talents, skills and experience through the text and the illustrations. Your brand identity is more subtle, but no less important. Imagine you are a medical specialist who cures back injuries. The Magician may be your natural archetype. We are not advocating a photograph of you wearing a pointed hat and waving a wand. However, your website will be more powerful if the vocabulary and content evoke the Magician. You could include a page of tips for people you have cured, to help them stay healthy. This will reinforce the message that you make the problem disappear and never return. If you use Magical words, such as *transform*, it will help to strengthen your brand identity.

If you are a fitness coach or personal trainer, the Hero is an obvious archetype for you to evoke on your website. You could have pictures of muscular men and women straining every sinew in pursuit of glory. However, that may not reflect what you do for your clients. Many people hire a personal trainer to make them stick to an exercise regime, so they lose weight and get fit. In other words, they want the Ruler. You could evoke the Ruler by having pictures of slim, athletic men and women in suits, striding up the steps to the entrance of a large corporation, with an architrave supported by Doric columns. You could include guidelines for healthy eating and exercise planners that people can download from your website.

If appropriate, you can mention your existing clients. The stronger their brands, the more yours will benefit. Links to other websites are crucial. They give people a reason to keep visiting your site and use it as a point of reference. When linking your website to others, make sure the connection enhances your brand. The quality of the sites, and the values they express, should be consistent with your own.

The more useful you make your website, the more likely people are to add it to their favourites list. You can also set up a site for a particular project. Clifford Thurlow did this when he wrote a book called *Making Short Films*. The website has become popular among media students and would-be filmmakers (see www.making-short-films.com). It has also increased the traffic on Clifford's own site.

Unless you are an accomplished web designer, you will need professional help with your site. However, there is no need to go overboard. Time-consuming animation can be counterproductive, since many people find it annoying. If they cannot *skip intro*, they may give up and go elsewhere. It helps to include third-party endorsements and articles that mention you.

The text is really important. Since this is a personal site, you can adopt an informal style that reflects the way you speak. It will help your personality to come across.

You can set up a website with a blog free of charge at www.word-press.com. This is an easy way to get started. However, it does have certain limitations. If you are technically inclined, you can build your own website and blog by going to www.workpress.org and downloading the 'open-source' (GPLv2 licensed) version of the software. This has lots of features and is very flexible. You will need to pay for a domain name and hosting. Alternatively, you can pay a web developer to tailor the software to your requirements. Since they will not have to build a website from scratch, this is much cheaper than the traditional approach, which used to cost thousands of pounds. These days, a presentable website with a blog and links to social media sites should cost only a few hundred pounds.

Ask someone to check the grammar and spelling. Then show a pilot version to a few people before it goes live. What is their first impression? How do they feel about what they see? Make sure your site is easy to navigate, so people keep coming back.

Once your site is up and running, it helps if people can find it quickly when they Google you. Your site's ranking will be determined by a number of factors that change from time to time. These include the number of links with other sites. You or your web designer can find out more about this in *Search Engine Optimization for Dummies,* which we have included under Recommended reading, page 235. If you are employed and appear on a corporate website, make sure it conveys the right message. If possible, check any material that mentions you before it goes live. Try printing out any pages that include your biography or photograph. The result may be very different from what you see on the screen. Photos can come out in many different sizes. Is your photo up-to-date and accurate? If you have aged 15 years or dyed your hair a different colour, it could cause embarrassment when you meet people face to face.

Here are some examples of good personal websites:

www.davidralphsimpson.com	Artist
www.karymullis.com	Biochemist
www.freyaillustration.co.uk	Cartoonist
www.neilmullarkey.com	Comedian
www.stelios.com	Entrepreneur and philanthropist
www.maxthurlow.com	Journalist
www.simonlaffin.com	Non-executive director
www.hawking.org.uk	Physicist
www.mitraalicetham.com	Pianist
www.sting.com	Singer/songwriter

Chapter

18

Using social media to build your brand

Communication on the internet used to be mainly one-way or two-way. We sent and received emails. Some of us had our own websites. There were no unusual branding issues so long as what you wrote was consistent with your purpose and evoked your preferred archetype. Group emails sent to large numbers of people took on a social dimension when recipients clicked on the 'reply all' button. However, this became an annoyance for many people. As their inboxes filled up, they began to ignore them.

In the meantime social interactions took place mainly offline: at home, at work, on the phone and in cafés, bars and restaurants. With the advent of social media, more and more of these interactions are taking place online, in front of hundreds, thousands or even millions of people. Just as with TV and radio, you can tune in and out whenever you want.

The implications of social media for personal branding are enormous. Relatively early in Twitter's development, a woman asked Deepak Chopra a question about dating: 'How do I find the perfect person?' His reply was: 'Be the perfect person.' This interaction was re-tweeted – i.e. forwarded – to at least 8 million people worldwide.

Making full use of social media

Understandably, there is confusion about how to use social media. Some sceptics say they have no interest in reading about what someone had for breakfast. Therefore the whole thing is a waste of time. However, the same could be said of radio, television and many newspapers and magazines. There is a torrent of information throughout the media, both on- and offline. The key is to clarify your message and find a way to connect with your audience.

As with anything new, we learn partly through trial and error. One common problem arises if you behave in one way online and in another way offline. You can end up evoking a wide range of archetypes and leaving people confused about who you really are.

Some people do things on social networking sites that they would never do elsewhere. For example, the wife of the head of MI6, Britain's secret service, posted a photo of him in his swimming trunks on Facebook, together with the address of their apartment and the whereabouts of their three children. The photo was then picked up by the press and widely circulated.

Social networking sites are like any other tool. They can be used well or badly. This book will help you do the former.

An introduction to social media

If you have completed the exercises in this book, you will have an understanding of yourself and the message you want to put across. In order to communicate effectively online, it helps to understand the media in question. In this chapter we will focus on blogs, Facebook, Google+, LinkedIn, Twitter and YouTube. Here is a brief description of each, in the order in which they have developed.

Blogs

Blog is short for *weblog*: effectively an online diary located on a website. Blogs first appeared in the late 1990s. Bloggers write text, sometimes accompanied by pictures, videos and audio recordings. People who read your blog can choose to subscribe to it. They will then receive new material via email or RSS (popularly known as Really Simple Syndication), which sends it to their computer or mobile phone. They can also leave comments on your blog, which you can either approve or reject. Readers are particularly likely to subscribe if you offer them some free material in return.

You can set up a blog for free on sites such as Wordpress (www.wordpress.com) and Blogger (www.blogger.com). However, if you want to build a strong personal brand online, it is often better to host your blog on your own website with your own domain, i.e. a website name that does not include the name of the blogging software. This shows that you are making a serious commitment to your blog and your online presence in general. It also gives you more flexibility. You can design the blog the way you want it, or pay someone else to do so. Having your own domain also makes it easier for you or someone you nominate to improve your ranking on Google and elsewhere using search engine optimisation (SEO).

You can use websites such as Digg, Facebook, Google+, LinkedIn, Pinterest, Reddit, StumbleUpon and Twitter to promote your blog. Stumbleupon has recently surpassed Facebook in terms of driving the most US Web traffic to social media sites. The *For Dummies* series, published by John Wiley & Sons, has several books on blogging that will help you get started.

Many people have made good use of blogs to establish and maintain a connection with their fans, clients, customers or investors. Some also sell products directly from their websites. The following examples may give you some ideas for your own blog:

bipling.com: Bip Ling, model, disc jockey and fashion blogger.

blog.guykawasaki.com: Guy Kawasaki, businessman, investor and author.

businesschic.com.au: Cheryl Lyn, stylist and photographer.

chrisbrogan.com: Chris Brogan, blogger, consultant and speaker.

dambisamoyo.com: Dambisa Moyo, author and economist.

goop.com: Gwyneth Paltrow, actress.

jeffbeck.com: Jeff Beck, guitarist.

notsalmon.com: Karen Salmansohn, author and broadcaster.

orangette.blogspot.com: Molly Wizenberg, food blogger and author.

paulaschoice.co.uk: Paula Begoun, skincare and cosmetics expert.

perezhilton.com: Perez Hilton, gossip columnist.

sethgodin.typepad.com: Seth Godin, marketing guru and author.

stephenfry.com: Stephen Fry, actor, author, television presenter and film director.

terrysmithblog.com: Terry Smith, chief executive and fund manager.

whatsthejackanory.com: Andrew Hetherington, photographer.

As you will see from the list above, celebrities often use their full names for their websites and blogs. This makes sense if they have already built a big brand offline. Their fans can then find them easily online.

If you happen not to be a celebrity, you may find that you can build a bigger and more valuable following by focusing on a subject that you are enthusiastic about. It is best if there is a clear benefit to visiting your blog, such as entertainment, useful information or solutions to a particular kind of problem. For example, at www.brandyou.info we focus on helping people to discover who they are and how they can best express themselves through their personal brands. We also give examples of people who have already done so successfully. The website works well for us in many respects: it enables us to keep in touch with our readers; it also gives potential clients a flavour of what we do and how we see things.

Whether your website is focused on you or on a particular topic, it helps to have an 'About' page, with a description of who you are and what you do – and a photograph in which you come across as friendly and approachable. Chris Brogan inserts pictures of himself in the text of his blog, for the same reason. A short video of you can be even more powerful. You can post it on YouTube and then embed it in your website or blog posts.

One proven way to build a following for your blog is to create great content and build relationships with other people who blog on closely related subjects. You can start by commenting (intelligently) on their blogs. Later on you may link your websites to each other. You can interview or be interviewed by them. You can write guest posts on each other's blogs. It is rather like television channels whose ratings are determined partly by the people who agree to appear on particular chat shows. Being controversial online often pays off. People love to listen to someone with a contrary opinion.

Once your blog is popular, you can use search engine optimisation (SEO) to help people find it. This means improving its ranking when people search on related topics using Google, for example. Even the headlines you use on your blog will affect its ranking. If you include keywords that people are likely to enter as search terms, they are more likely to find your blog. You can either invest the necessary time and energy to learn SEO, or you can hire someone who is already an expert on the subject. It is best not to use SEO before you have built a following. Otherwise Google may blacklist your blog.

Starting a blog is a commitment, since it should normally be updated at least once a week to be effective. (Google likes fresh content.) Some people update their blogs 3–5 times per week. It gives their readers a reason to keep coming back for new posts.

If you only update your blog occasionally, it may become more like an online brochure. In this case it is worth ensuring that all the content is accurate, both factually and grammatically, just like any other brochure. It is also helpful to include 'share' buttons that enable people to tell their friends about your blog on the main social networking sites described below.

The more strongly your blog evokes a particular archetype, the easier it will be to build a following. A blog can be a great place to publish and test new ideas, which you can then turn into a book. Those who subscribe to the blog are likely to buy your book and/or recommend it to others. Seth Godin has published 13 books based on his regular posts at www.sethgodin.typepad.com

LinkedIn (2003, www.linkedin.com)

This site has a very corporate feel to it, partly due to its design and colour scheme. LinkedIn describes itself as a professional network rather than a social one. Many companies allow their employees to use it at work. On average, two new people join every second.

Communication theorist Marshall McLuhan famously said that 'the medium is the message'. In other words, the form of a medium embeds itself in the message and affects how the message is perceived. That is certainly true of LinkedIn. If all you do is fill in the boxes and upload your CV, you are likely to evoke the Ruler by default. The structure, layout and colour scheme are exactly what you would expect of a site populated primarily by managers. If you want to evoke another archetype, you may need to do something more original.

LinkedIn's groups are very popular. Other visitors to the website can see the groups you belong to, which can have an effect on your brand. It is usually best to join a small number that relate directly to the work you do – or aspire to. As ever, plugging yourself or your business may be counterproductive. If you contribute intelligent, high-quality questions or answers to some of the discussions, it will help to position you as someone who is active and/or interested in this particular field. LinkedIn also enables you to describe any event you may be organising and invite people to it.

The 'Recommendations' section can be effective, if you use it in the right way. Many headhunters are understandably cynical, since it is easy for people to club together and recommend each other. The most credible recommendations are from former clients and bosses, i.e. people who have paid you to work for them. Short recommendations are good. Visitors to your page are much more likely to read them. It is best to have no more than ten recommendations, from bosses, clients, professors and others. We suggest you avoid recommendations from friends, since they make you look less credible.

Recruitment consultants increasingly use LinkedIn as a back-up database. If they do not already have a candidate's CV or contact details, they can usually find them on LinkedIn. Make sure the dates, job titles, etc. on your LinkedIn profile match those on the CV that you give to potential employers. Elsewhere on LinkedIn it is good to talk about what you *want* to do and not just what you *have* done.

However, if all you do is transcribe your CV onto LinkedIn and upload a photo of yourself in business attire, you risk being two-dimensional. Instead of your brand being a tall, distinctive building that is visible for miles around, it will be one of those grey ones that almost no one notices as they go past.

You are likely to write a much better explanation of who you are on LinkedIn once you have read *Brand You* and have done the exercises. Then you will understand your brand in depth. You can explain what you do, how you do it and what you want to do.

As we mentioned in Chapter 9, it is best to summarise what you do in one short, memorable phrase. For example, instead of describing yourself as 'Marketing Manager at Whizzo Media', you might write 'Digital marketing specialist for high-growth media companies'. People need to know what you do, which is not the same thing as your job title. Your headline is probably the most important section of your profile.

LinkedIn adds new features all the time, partly in response to competition from other websites. The 'Skills' section in your profile is particularly useful, since it is close to the unique combination of talents, skills and experience that we discussed in Chapter 9. You can choose them from a drop-down menu. For example:

John Purkiss:

executive search, personal branding, personal development, author

David Royston-Lee:

career strategy, personal branding, psychology, published author, executive coaching, leadership mentoring

Pay particular attention to the 'Keywords' section. It enables recruitment firms, as well as potential employers and clients, to find you by searching the entire LinkedIn database swiftly.

You can add other material, such as SlideShare presentations, documents, videos and your latest blog posts. All of these can help to create the right impression when people visit your LinkedIn page.

It is worth thinking about who you are going to add to your network on LinkedIn. If you are a professional serving a tightly defined market, you may wish to focus on a particular group of people. If you have a much wider market – as an author or speaker, for example – then you may decide to connect with everyone who wants to connect with you.

Facebook (2004, www.facebook.com)

Facebook started out as a purely social website for students at Harvard University. It is now the largest social networking site in the world, in terms of the number of users. However, it has also become important in business. Increasingly, employers and potential business partners will look at your Facebook page. It is likely to come up when they search for you on Google.

Some people prefer to use Facebook purely for their personal and social lives. However, some of us win business through the website, which is gradually becoming more professional and career-oriented. A significant percentage of our new clients are the friends, clients or acquaintances of people we keep in touch with online. This is unsurprising if you imagine Facebook as the online equivalent of a café or other social venue in the centre of a town or city. If people bump into you now and then, and are clear about what you do for a living, they are bound to think of you whenever they need your services or talk to someone else who does. Software applications such as BranchOut ('Professional networking on Facebook') are taking the site further into LinkedIn's traditional territory.

One of Facebook's advantages is that it enables people to build up a picture of you over several weeks, months or years. They can read your posts, watch your videos and look at other people's material when you share it. All of this helps to build your brand.

Facebook has groups, just like LinkedIn. Facebook Groups allow you to share pictures, videos and links just as you can within a normal account. However, it all takes place within the group. It is also very easy to send a message to other members of the group. Just like LinkedIn, Facebook enables you to describe any event you may be organising and invite people to it. You can also set up a Facebook Page for your business. A Facebook Page may prove particularly useful if you want to build a large following. Facebook limits the number of friends you can have on your profile to 5,000. A Page has no limit.

One of the most useful aspects of Facebook is the discussion strings. If you post something that people find entertaining or thought-provoking, some of them will start to make comments in the box provided. You may be able to answer their questions or help solve their problems. Sometimes lengthy discussions may develop, with or without you. Some people prefer simply to indicate that they like your post. Either way, you get rapid feed-back. Some people use this to test ideas for products, services or books. It is like an online focus group, free of charge.

Facebook is particularly effective if your work or other interests involve either static or moving images. You can upload the latter via YouTube, described below.

If you naturally evoke the Sage, you can do so by sharing useful material you have come across in your area of expertise. However, it is all too easy to re-post other people's material all the time. You then risk being seen as someone who has nothing original to say. It is better to add your own opinions and comments to stories, videos, photos and quotations.

YouTube (2005, www.youtube.com)

This is a useful personal branding tool for people in a wide range of occupations. If you are paid as a speaker, actor or musician, potential clients will be able to see you perform. If you are a film-maker, you can upload short examples of your work. A wide range of people find it helpful to embed YouTube videos in their websites, so viewers can get a sense of who they are while they are delivering their message. Chris Brogan does this to great effect at www.chrisbrogan.com.

People have launched successful careers on YouTube, sometimes from their bedrooms. The singer/songwriter Justin Bieber began by putting his videos on YouTube. In 2008 he was discovered by Scooter Braun, who later became his manager. Bieber released his second studio album *Under the Mistletoe* in November 2011. It entered the Billboard 200 chart at number one.

If you use a search engine, such as Google, videos often appear on the front page. It is worth bearing in mind that YouTube is owned by Google. Rather than always writing text for your blog, you may prefer to make a video and insert it into your blog. This has several advantages:

- Videos help people to grasp who you are as a person. They will relate to you more easily and feel more comfortable doing business with you. Some people find videos far more engaging than photographs or text.

- If you are an expert on a particular subject and upload videos of yourself speaking to live audiences, you are likely to receive invitations to speak elsewhere. Becoming a professional speaker can boost your income as well as strengthening your brand in terms of both reach and reputation.

- It gives you another way to engage with your audience. Some people prefer to watch a video rather than read about what you do.

- YouTube is also a great tool for researching any subject that interests you. Experts often upload their latest presentations at conferences around the globe.

A video can be a powerful addition to your blog or page on a social networking site. You can, of course, have one made professionally. However, many people make their own videos in their home or office and then embed them in their websites. Increasingly, digital cameras have a 'movie' function, so you may already have the necessary equipment. Here are some tips to help you and anyone who is working with you on your video:

- Choose your clothes carefully. It is a good idea to avoid striped shirts or blouses, since they can cause distracting visual effects. It is safer to wear a plain colour that is flattering to your skin tone.

- Decide what you want to include or exclude in the background. Bookshelves may evoke the Sage. Is that what you intend? If you are making the video out of doors, will there be any distractions in the background?

- Use the 'white balance' function. Otherwise your video may come out very blue or red for no apparent reason. The white balance function allows you to adjust the 'colour temperature' according to the lighting conditions where you are filming. The four main categories are: sunlight, shade on a sunny day, cloudy day and electric light. If you get the white balance right, the colours in the final video will appear more natural.

- Choose the right focal length. The 'neutral' focal length, in terms of 35 mm photography, is 50 mm. As you reduce the focal length below 50 mm it becomes easier to keep everything in focus. You will also include more of the background in the frame. However, there is a danger that your face will be distorted if you get too close to the lens. As you increase the focal length above 50 mm it is easier to ensure that only you appear in the frame. The background will start to become blurred. However, so will you if the lens is not focused accurately.

Having said all this, the key to video is to start doing it. You can tweak the style and format as you go along. Chris Brogan records videos from his office. They may not look very polished, but they enable viewers to understand who he is and relate to him. As a result he has hundreds of thousands of followers.

We have found that being interviewed – or participating in a face-to-face discussion – on video has many advantages:

- A conversation is often more engaging for viewers than a solo broadcast.
- Interesting new ideas often emerge unexpectedly.
- Humour and anecdotes come naturally during a conversation.

Twitter (2006, www.twitter.com)

This is a 'microblogging' site. When you write a *tweet* you can use a maximum of 140 characters, although web addresses beginning with http: and www. are automatically shortened. One reason so many people follow Twitter is that it is more up-to-date than conventional news. You can also search to see which topics are 'trending', i.e. being discussed by millions of people worldwide. For example, when Michael Jackson died many of those who commented on the event inserted a *hashtag* into their tweets. #michaeljackson was number one on Twitter Trends, closely followed by #michealjackson.

You can use hashtags to find people who share your interests and communicate with them online. For example, if you play or write about rock music, you can search for tweets that mention #rockmusic. If you then tweet on the subject, you can also insert #rockmusic. Here is an example:

U2 were great on TV last night. Meanwhile, we're rehearsing for our gig at the Dog & Duck this Friday. #rockmusic

You can invent or use any hashtag you like. For example, if you search on #BrandYou you will see tweets by John and David, as well as many other people, some of whom are writing about personal branding in general, rather than about this book.

You can download free software on the Web that connects your Twitter account to LinkedIn. This enables you to copy a tweet from Twitter to LinkedIn simply by inserting #in into the tweet. For example, John could write the following:

David and I enjoyed running a #BrandYou seminar at London Metropolitan University last night. Good questions from the students. #in

This tweet will then appear automatically in John's LinkedIn feed, where all his contacts on that site will be able to read it.

One of Twitter's innovations is 'asymmetric relationships', i.e. users can follow others without requiring them to follow back. Hence some celebrities follow a few people but have many more followers of their own. In most cases you need no permission to follow someone on Twitter. Twitter is particularly powerful for people such as journalists, politicians, actors, singers and gurus of all types. When Laura Kuenssberg, the BBC's chief political correspondent, moved to ITV, her new employer said that her 60,000 Twitter followers were an 'additional benefit' in hiring her. Barack Obama (@barackobama) and Stephen Fry (@stephenfry) have millions of followers on Twitter.

Some organisations forbid their employees to make comments on Twitter for fear that they will be interpreted as the organisation's point of view. This is a natural concern in industries such as financial services, which are highly regulated. However, that should not necessarily prevent you from following other people on Twitter. For example, if you are a spokesperson for your organisation, you can follow the journalists who regularly interview you and write about your employer. This will help you to build a stronger rapport with them. An easy way to do this is to download Twitter's software application (or 'app') onto your smartphone.

Among all the social media tools, Twitter has the greatest reach. Anyone anywhere can read your tweets and get in touch. It is a very good place to make contact with new people. You can then connect with them on LinkedIn, Facebook and your blog, or by email.

As with any other media, on- or offline, it is essential that what you write on Twitter fits your purpose/mission and the archetype(s) you intend to evoke. For example, John mainly evokes the Magician and the Jester on Twitter. He rarely evokes the Lover or the Outlaw. You can use your preferred archetypes as a guide to what you tweet about and how you tweet it. It is just like a newspaper or TV station's editorial policy. Once you are clear about that, you can tweet about anything you like. You will quickly discover what people find attractive or boring, by the way they respond to your tweets. It is best not to tweet continuously about your business or the particular project you are working on; but do mention it now and then, ideally with a hashtag, so that people can find it again easily. However, just as in any conversation, it is best to discuss a wide range of topics that interest you.

Some people treat Twitter as a broadcast medium, like TV or radio. That is fine if you are a celebrity with a seemingly endless supply of jokes or a fascinating 'private' life. However, most of us find Twitter far more productive and useful if we treat it as a conversation. When someone says something you find interesting or amusing, you can reply to them using the @ key. All your followers will be able to see what you have written. The person to whom you are responding will also receive an alert, so they can continue the conversation. For example, after John's tweet shown on page 192 above, David might reply by saying:

@JohnPurkiss Interesting that only one student at #LondonMet wasn't on Facebook. They seemed to like the idea of personal websites.

Other people who read this tweet can join in the conversation simply by using @JohnPurkiss and/or @DavidRoystonLee, as they see fit. For example, a student might write:

@JohnPurkiss @DavidRoystonLee Thanks for the seminar! Can we do more on personal websites next time? We're working on that at #LondonMet.

By interacting with people on Twitter in this way, you can communicate with a large number of people who share your interests and build new connections.

Google+ (2011, www.plus.google.com)

This site has combined some of the best features of Facebook, LinkedIn and Twitter, while attempting to resolve a few of their drawbacks. The layout is rather like a blog with several contributors, including you.

Every time you add someone to your Google+ contacts you can allocate them to one or more 'circles'. Ready-made circles include *family*, *friends* and *following*. You can delete these if you wish. You can also create others such as *colleagues*, *clients*, *investors* or *fans*. Your contacts know they are in one or more of your circles, but they do not know which ones. When you post on Google+, you can decide which circles are going to receive your post. More importantly, you can decide which circles are *not* going to receive it. This enables you to separate the material that your personal and professional contacts see.

Google+ is fully integrated with the other free software applications on Google, as well as the search engine itself.

Chapter

19

Getting started with social media

To get started with social media, we suggest you do the following right away:

1 Purchase a domain name with your full name, if it is available, e.g. www.johnpurkiss.com, www.davidroystonlee.com. You can always use it to redirect people elsewhere.

2 If you have not already done so, open accounts on Facebook, Google+, LinkedIn and Twitter, even if you have no immediate plans to use them. You may end up using only one or two of them. However, you may at some point want to use all four, in which case it will be helpful to have the same name across all the main platforms.

3 Use your first name and surname if they are available. If not, choose an online name that is easily recognisable as you and can be used for both personal and professional purposes across all social networking sites. Consistency will help people to find you and connect with you easily.

4 Secure the 'vanity URL' (unique resource locator) for your online name on all four websites. This is the URL that includes your name, for example:

https://www.facebook.com/JohnPurkiss

https://www.facebook.com/davidroystonlee

https://twitter.com/#!/johnpurkiss

https://twitter.com/#!/davidroystonlee

On LinkedIn and Twitter this will happen automatically when you open your account. On Facebook and Google+ you may wish to ask a friend who has more experience to help you. Once you have done this, it is much easier to send people to the appropriate page on the Web, e.g. www.facebook.com/johnpurkiss instead of www.facebook.com/e2434h394oij.

5 Complete your Google+ and LinkedIn profiles. All you need right now is the basic information. Once your profile is up and running, it will improve your Google ranking when people

search for you online. In the bio you can include hyperlinks to your pages on other sites, such as Facebook, LinkedIn, Twitter and YouTube, as well as to your blog. You can choose which part of your profile is visible from a random search on Google and which part is visible only to your friends and family, for example.

6 Get a professional head-and-shoulders photo that you can use on all websites. While you are about it, it is worth asking for some with plain white backgrounds. Editors of other websites will find them useful if they write an article about you.

Think about who you are trying to reach

Depending on your security settings, anyone anywhere in the world could be reading what you write online. You may wish to ignore this fact and write purely for your local market, or for a group of people who share your outlook and/or interests. However, if you are targeting a global market, it is worth considering cultural differences.

In some cultures it is considered normal and acceptable to promote yourself and tell everyone how great you are. In others this is considered boastful and rude, so people with much to offer are silent and practically invisible on the Web. If you find yourself at either extreme, you may wish to adapt your style and move closer to the middle. Then you can appeal to a global audience.

If you build a large following online, it is rather like having your own TV or radio station. When you go to meetings or social events, people will comment on what you have written online and the discussions that have arisen out of it. You may discover that people read more of your material online than you had realised – they may simply choose not to comment on it.

Keep up to date

Online personal branding is developing fast. Here are some websites that will help you to learn more and keep up to date:

www.brandyou.info

www.chrisbrogan.com

www.executivecareerbrand.com

www.socialmediaexaminer.com

www.thepersonalbrandingblog.com

www.theundercoverrecruiter.com

Succeeding with social media

As in any market, there is more than one potentially successful strategy. Here are some examples of what works.

Twitter/blog/email/Amazon

John Locke is an entrepreneur and author. He gets to know people on Twitter and encourages them to visit his blog. Some of them then sign up for his emails, which alert them when his next book is published. He has built a big online following this way and has become the first self-published author to sell 1 million e-books on Amazon's Kindle: www.donovancreed.com.

Perpetual tweeting

This approach can work well for celebrities, i.e. people who are already famous. Examples include politicians, television personalities, comedians and writers. They need to stay visible and keep people's attention. For decades they have done this through interviews in the press and appearances on television chat shows.

However, Twitter goes a big step further by enabling them to engage with their fans and have discussions with them. Some use Twitter to test-market new ideas which may then become books, products or businesses. Here are some examples of successful users of Twitter:

@BarackObama

@chrisbrogan

@DalaiLama

@DeepakChopra

@MayorOfLondon

@stephenfry

Building a community around your blog

Andrew Hetherington is a photographer who was born in Britain and lives in New York. We mentioned his blog earlier: www. whatsthejackanory.com. The strap line is 'another fine hetherington™ photo product quality guaranteed'.

Andrew writes about his photographic adventures and about other photographers he knows and admires. Some of them are famous. He often meets them when they are passing through New York. There is a link to his personal website and portfolio, which helps him to win new assignments: www.ahetherington.com.

From blog to group on Facebook/LinkedIn

Once people arrive at your blog, some will be happy to comment in the space provided below each post. Others will feel more comfortable commenting within a group on Facebook or LinkedIn. For example, on www.brandyou.info we invite people to join the discussion in the *Brand You* group on Facebook. All are welcome.

If your blog turns into a book, a product, a service or an organisation, you can set up a Page on Facebook. People who click on the 'like' button on your Page will then see your updates whenever you post them. *Brand You* has a Facebook Page, too.

From blog to book(s) and speaking engagements

Seth Godin is known internationally as a marketing guru. He regularly turns material that he has published on www.sethsblog.com into books. There are now more than a dozen of them. His blog tells you about his books and his availability for speaking engagements. It also has a link to his main website, www.sethgodin.com.

From YouTube to television and a record deal

As we mentioned earlier, it worked for Justin Bieber. Sir Ken Robinson is less of a celebrity and more of an expert on education. His talks on the subject at TED (www.ted.com) have attracted nearly 6 million visitors. Like us, he believes everyone should concentrate on what they are good at and enjoy doing.

Tips to help you fine-tune your approach

Using a new medium always involves a certain amount of trial and error. One of the advantages of social media is that you get rapid feedback. If you do something on Facebook that people like, some will tell you so. If they do not like it, or you are posting too frequently, some will 'unfriend' you.

Here are some further tips:

- Do not put the following information on a social networking site: your date and place of birth, travel plans or home address.
- You can save yourself a lot of time and anxiety if you assume that anything you post online is public. Even if you post something among friends and family with maximum security settings, someone can still cut and paste what you have written and post it anywhere they want on the Web.

■ If you are going to use Facebook for professional purposes, it is best not to play online games, unless they are relevant to your work as a game developer or marketer, for example. If people see you playing games online, some of them may conclude that you are not very busy or that you find your work boring.

■ It is good to talk about your hobbies and other interests. You will connect with some people right away when you discover you have something in common outside work. It also shows that you are not two-dimensional and/or a geek.

■ Talk about your business, product or service only now and then. It is best to spend at least 90 per cent of your time providing material that your audience will enjoy, without trying to sell them anything. It is rather like commercial television – an advertisement now and then is acceptable; if there are too many of them, people get bored and switch off.

■ It is often best to entertain or inform people, with periodic mentions of your main topic. For example, on Facebook you can share jokes, videos or photos, provided they fit the archetypes that you evoke normally. For example, if you have decided that your archetypes include the Jester but not the Outlaw, you will probably decide to include clean jokes but not dirty ones.

■ Having said this, it is important to stand out, which may mean taking risks from time to time. You may occasionally tread on someone's toes by accident. All you can do is apologise and move on. If you are sincere about serving people – rather than criticising – most of them will understand.

■ It is much easier to stand out if you write and speak authentically. In other words, you should be yourself in all media and in real life. People will warm to you if they can see what they perceive as your faults as well as your good points. The psychologist Carl Jung said: 'I'd rather be whole than good.' If you think about the most successful people in the conventional media, such as musicians, sportspeople, broadcasters and film stars, their fans are all too aware of their failings. However, they love them all the same. Most of us relate to people who are human rather than perfect and therefore artificial.

- It is usually better to write from the point of view of an expert or fellow explorer of a particular subject, rather than a pushy promoter of a product or service. Ken Robinson, mentioned above, is an example of the former. It is fine to mention whatever you are selling now and then. If you are writing on your blog, you can even include an advertisement and a 'buy now' button. We suggest the aim of building your brand online is to engage with people and make sure they remember you when they have a need that you may be able to meet. In the meantime, you want them to keep coming back to you online for free updates.

- Make sure what you say is true and accurate. Would you be comfortable saying it to a complete stranger the first time you met them?

- Get the heading right on each website. You can vary the style a bit according to the medium, while keeping the content the same. For example, 'Consultant in Executive Search & Personal Brand Strategy' on LinkedIn becomes 'Headhunter and Personal Brand Strategist' on Facebook. Recruiters will find you when they search on key words.

- Participate constructively in LinkedIn groups, particularly those that are open to Google search.

- Comment on blogs in your field. You can usually tell which are the most popular by looking at the number of retweets, shares and blog comments. Popular blogs automatically get a high Google ranking. Having said all of this, when you are commenting on other people's blogs, the priority is to build a relationship with the bloggers and their contacts.

- When people comment on your posts or your blog, be sure to reply to their comments, where appropriate. Some people treat social media like old-fashioned broadcasting: they send their message out into the world and then ignore what anyone says in response. This can make them look out of touch or arrogant. It is much better to engage with your audience and acknowledge them. If you are helpful and sincere, you can build a relationship with some of them. Your following will begin to grow. This is especially true on your blog. When you reply to people's comments, a virtuous circle develops, making your blog look and become more and more popular.

- Comment on other people's posts with care. On the one hand, they generally like it when you read what they write and respond constructively, or with humour. On the other hand, if you are going to evoke the Jester – with cheeky humour – it may be better to send them a direct message that other people cannot see. Otherwise they may take offence at being laughed at in front of their friends.

- Post on Facebook only once or twice a day. Make sure it is something of widespread interest. If you post more often, you may start to lose followers, particularly those with few Facebook friends who discover you are hogging their screen. You will become like the person at a party who talks all the time. If you post something and no one reacts to it within an hour, you can always remove it and post something else.

- Use Twitter, Facebook, LinkedIn and Google+ to invite people to visit your blog and then join your mailing list.

- Share other people's material selectively, i.e. only if it is consistent with your archetype and what you want to be known for.

- If someone criticises you online, by all means reply, but avoid getting into an online argument that everyone can see.

- Be a trend-setter in your community/industry. Write original content.

- When you produce original content, put it on as many sites as possible.

- Support causes that fit your brand and your preferred archetype. You can pursue your purpose more effectively as a member of a group.

- It is part of the etiquette on Facebook not to post photographs of people without their permission. If someone does this to you, especially if they 'tag' you by attaching your name to a photo, you can ask them to remove it. If they persist, you can 'unfriend' them and/or report them to Facebook.

- If you use the same head-and-shoulders photo of yourself on all social media sites, it will be easier for people to find you and connect with you. Some men prefer to wear a jacket and tie in their photo on LinkedIn.

Measuring the results

The way you measure the results of your social media strategy depends on what you do and what you are aiming to achieve. If you are a politician, journalist or other public figure, you may wish to use a service such as Klout (www.klout.com). If you are writing a blog, you can monitor your visitors using Google Analytics, for example. This service shows you the number of visits your website has received each day, which pages were viewed and whether people visited your site directly or via a search engine or referral site. Google Analytics also enables you to see each visitor's country of origin.

Chapter

20

Becoming famous

A large following can bring you many opportunities. People in music, sport and cinema have achieved international fame and used it to extend their brands into new markets. A much larger number have done this on a national scale. Alan Sugar built up Amstrad, a consumer electronics company in the UK. He has since chaired Tottenham Hotspur Football Club and become a major property investor. He is also the star of *The Apprentice* on BBC TV, a role played by Donald Trump in the US. Some people are rarely seen in the national media, but are well known internationally in their sector. Dr Barry Cohen is a US plastic surgeon who has written books, launched his own range of skin-care products and opened a chain of clinics on both sides of the Atlantic. See www.bjcohen.com and www.beyondmedispa.com.

Famous face or famous name?

What kind of fame would help you or hold you back? Some people are recognised wherever they go. This may help if you are a model, an actor or a television personality. At the very least you will get better tables in restaurants. Singers such as Sting and Bono have used their fame to lobby for environmental causes or social change.

However, fame can have its disadvantages, most obviously the loss of freedom. You may have to pay extra on planes and in hotels just to keep away from the general public. You may need a bodyguard to go shopping or attend a social event. Relationships become more complicated if people want to be seen with you.

Some people have a famous name but not a well-known face. Johannes Vermeer, one of the best-known painters of the Dutch Golden Age, only painted himself from behind. We have little idea what he looked like. Doris Lessing is a Nobel Prize-winning novelist, but few people would recognise her in the street.

It helps to have a famous relative, particularly if they evoke the same archetype as you. Stella McCartney's career as a fashion designer has benefited from Paul McCartney's brand. They both evoke the Creator. Roger Bannister is known as the first man to run a mile in less than four minutes, thereby evoking the Hero. His son Clive has pursued a career in finance, most recently as a senior executive with HSBC and now chief executive of Phoenix, an insurance company. His father's Heroic achievement is usually mentioned whenever Clive is interviewed in the press. It is part of his heritage and helps to strengthen his brand.

Do you want to be a celebrity?

The dictionary definition of celebrity is being famous in your lifetime. However, it has also come to mean being famous for being famous.

Celebrity status is fine if you have built your brand on your talents and values. It will give you extra momentum in pursuit of your purpose. Al Gore's political career provided a launch pad for his campaign to combat global warming. As he said in his speeches: 'My name's Al Gore. I used to be the next president of the United States.' Many celebrities become famous without discovering a particular talent or identifying their purpose. Many of them evoke the Ordinary Guy or Girl and people feel they are 'just like us'. They charge lower fees than talented celebrities, helping to make reality television highly profitable. Unfortunately, thousands of others can do the same. It is hard to build a long-term career on this basis.

Staying famous can require effort, but even traumatic events may help, provided you evoke your archetype consistently. Some successful actors and singers evoke the Outlaw. They break the rules, even at the expense of their health. If they spend time in rehab at The Priory or the Betty Ford Clinic, it helps to sustain their fans' interest in them. Although these establishments charge a lot for medical treatment, the publicity is exceptionally good value. Once the media latch onto a story about drugs or alcohol, it reaches millions of people. We are not suggesting you do the same. However, you may find other creative ways to evoke your archetype.

It is sometimes said that all publicity is good publicity. We disagree. Publicity is only good if it fits your purpose. A famous example is Gerald Ratner, the former chief executive of the Ratners jewellery chain, which he built up from 130 stores to 2,500 over a period of ten years. In 1991 he told a conference that a sherry decanter sold by his company was 'total crap'. His remark wiped £500 million off the value of the company, which swung from a large profit to a large loss. That remark also cost him his job.

It might have been better for the chief executive of a public company to evoke the Ruler. Another helpful archetype would have been the Ordinary Guy/Girl, since Ratners made gold jewellery accessible to people on moderate incomes. By denigrating his company's products he evoked the Outlaw, with destructive consequences for both the company and his career. He has since made a comeback with geraldonline.com, a large online jewellery business.

How famous do you want to be?

Being famous will help you when you attend a meeting or social event, or appear in the media. People will feel they know you. However, you must also be *authentic* – true to your values and your purpose. Then there will be no surprises as you build new relationships.

Few names or faces are recognised worldwide, and most of us do not need that level of recognition. It is better to define the group you want to reach and become famous among *them*. Who do you want to recognise you? It could be a few thousand people in your country. It could be those who work in your sector, in several countries. Once you have defined your target audience, you can think about how to reach them. Ideally you should use several media at once. As we mentioned in Chapter 1, when people have heard about you in three different ways, you begin to stand out in their minds.

Chapter

21

Protecting and extending your brand

Although your brand is an *intangible* asset, it could easily become more valuable than any *physical* asset you possess. It is therefore worth protecting.

Managing your brand name(s)

The steps you take to protect your personal brand name will partly depend on how famous you are, or intend to become. If you decide to be visible on the Web, it is best to register your domain name both as a .com and using your local suffix. For example: john-purkiss.com and johnpurkiss.co.uk. This can be hard if your name is a common one. You can check whether your name is available by visiting a site such as freeparking.com. It is easier if you have an unusual nickname. For example, Gordon Sumner became known as Sting because he wore a black-and-yellow striped sweater that made him look like a wasp. (See sting.com.) You may even be able to register your name and logo as a trademark.

Treat people fairly

New ventures are always risky, whether they are in the theatre, the cinema, technology, consumer products, retailing or elsewhere. However, you can ensure that everyone involved knows the risks they are taking and is treated fairly. You can also make sure, before you take on a project, that you have the time and resources required to do an excellent job. If you have to cancel the whole thing, or close down a business, you can do so ethically and transparently.

Some people damage their brands without thinking about it. They gain in the short term but lose in the long term. If you behave impeccably, you will keep attracting people and new opportunities. You will be much better off overall.

Take the initiative – deal with problems straight away

If your colleagues share your values, you should have few problems. However, if they do anything that could damage your brand, you may have to distance yourself. Turning a blind eye is a big risk. It may be enough to tell them how uncomfortable you feel about what is going on. The advantage of saying how you feel is that no one can contradict you. Neither have you judged them nor accused them of anything.

If they are doing something illegal, it is worth consulting a lawyer. You may wish to resign or terminate your relationship. The longer you allow things to continue, the greater the potential damage to your brand. The business world and politics offer many examples of reputations and entire careers blighted by scandal. If it emerges that you acted swiftly when you found out what was going on, it may even *enhance* your brand.

Extending your brand

Brands are not single products or services. As we said in Chapter 2, a brand is a symbol that guarantees a particular experience. Brands give meaning to life and can take many forms. They can be extended to new products and services, provided the *essence* of the brand is maintained. As Andy Milligan points out in his book, *Brand It Like Beckham*: 'Once people experience a brand and like it, it acquires the legitimacy to offer them something else: maybe a different kind of product, but one with similarities in form or function or emotional resonance.'

Successful corporate brands have done this for many years. Virgin started as a record company. The brand has since been extended to air travel, financial services, mobile phones and many other products and services. The Easy brand has been extended from easyJet to easyCruise and beyond. Brands can be extended if they make and fulfil a strong promise to customers, with a consistent purpose and set of values. When the Virgin Group launches a new product or business, customers expect innovation, value for money and fun. If a brand keeps its promise, it becomes more valuable than before. Broken promises will damage it.

The same applies to your brand. If you are thinking of doing something new, ask yourself whether it will fit your purpose and your values. Will it evoke the same archetype as before? Leonardo da Vinci consistently evoked the Creator, whether he was painting portraits or designing flying machines. A modern example of the Creator is Philip Hughes, co-founder of Logica, the IT services company. He became known as a painter while he was still chairman. Since leaving the company he has pursued a full-time career as an artist.

Imagine your brand is a tall building with a large atrium. When visitors enter at street level, they immediately get a feel for its purpose. It might be a department store selling everything for the home. There are counters and shop assistants everywhere. When visitors look up, they see balconies on the floors above. Your department store can add any product range that is consistent with your purpose and your values.

It is best to extend your brand to areas where you are credible or can become so quickly. David has a background as a psychologist and was previously a human resources director, a chief executive and a management consultant. He now draws on all this experience to help organisations and their senior people to clarify their mission and market themselves more effectively.

John has used his knowledge of executive search and personal development to write books that help people in their careers. This has led to invitations to speak to large audiences and to assist senior executives with their personal brands. These activities fit naturally with his role as a headhunter.

Exercise U: Extending your brand

Write down, in as much detail as you can, everything you enjoy doing and do well. Include the things you do at work and in your spare time. What are the underlying talents? What are the values that make those activities meaningful for you? Write down all the other talents you have discovered in yourself and enjoy using, but are not using right now.

Now make a list of new activities you would like to try. Could you begin any of them now?

Experimenting with and extending your brand helps you maintain a high level of energy. It keeps you at the forefront of what interests you most.

David Beckham: a case study in brand extension

David Beckham is a good example of how to build a global brand and extend it beyond the original activity. The material in this case study is taken from Andy Milligan's book, *Brand It Like Beckham – The Story of How Brand Beckham Was Built*. If you are interested in personal branding and/or football, we highly recommend it.

Beckham has a strong element of the Magician. He may not be the greatest footballer the world has ever seen, but he is exceptionally skilful, often transforming his team's fortunes. He also evokes the Ordinary Guy consistently. This strengthens his appeal to people who feel that he is 'just like me'. He has built a unique brand that is admired around the world by men and women, young and old.

Beckham has benefited from major changes in his market. These include the rise of the English Premier League to international prominence, fuelled by revenues from terrestrial and satellite broadcasting. FIFA's decision to promote the game globally has greatly extended his international reach. The tournaments in the US in 1994 and Korea/Japan in 2002 helped to build an international market.

Some people turn their noses up at David Beckham. However, his critics will not be attracted to him anyway if the Ordinary Guy archetype does not appeal to them. The key to his success in building a global brand is that he has evoked the Magician and the Ordinary Guy consistently. This has enabled him to extend his brand across several product categories.

Here are some of the steps that have worked well for Beckham in building his personal brand:

- At the age of 16 he appointed an agent to look after his affairs. This enabled him to concentrate on improving his game.

- He signed with Manchester United, which has a tradition of stylish football and now has more fans in Asia than it does in the UK and Ireland.

- He has cultivated the brand values of dedication, style and down-to-earth honesty. They come across in everything he does, from his determination to be the best footballer he can, to the way he follows fashion and expresses his emotions openly.

- He is softly spoken and appears humble. This increases his appeal in Asian cultures that are founded on respect.

- His lack of fluency in his mother tongue is consistent with the Ordinary Guy and has made people warm to him. When asked by a journalist if he was learning Japanese in time for the 2002 World Cup, he replied: 'I'm still tryin' English.'

- His good looks have enabled him to extend his brand from football to fashion. In 2001 he launched the Police eyewear collection in the UK. This was the first campaign that did not draw on his image as a footballer, but promoted his looks and fashion sense instead.

- His marriage to former Spice Girl Victoria Adams gave him access to the world of entertainment and the tabloid press. She also took his surname, helping to spread the Beckham brand to a wider audience.

- He consistently pursues excellence, both on and off the field. Becoming England captain in 2000 brought him no direct commercial benefit, but the emotion and imagery surrounding the England brand, with its three-lion logo, have undoubtedly strengthened his own.

- In 2003 he moved from Manchester United to Real Madrid. His new club had an even greater heritage, reputation for style and record of achievement. At the time it was the most successful club in Europe. He was also awarded an OBE.

- He provided Real Madrid with a ready-made marketing channel into Asia, where he is widely revered. This was reflected in his contract, which included key clauses relating to image rights. The move also gave him access to the Hispanic market, with over 425 million native Spanish-speakers worldwide. Both he and Real Madrid were sponsored by Adidas, which made him more valuable to them.

- He and Victoria appointed the pop impresario Simon Fuller, who had launched the Spice Girls, to build the Beckham brand globally.

- In 2007 Beckham announced his decision to join LA Galaxy in Los Angeles. Having built a strong presence in the Spanish-speaking market during his time with Real Madrid, he was now well placed to develop his brand in the US. Hispanics represent around 15 per cent of the US population and have a keener interest in soccer than their non-Hispanic compatriots.

- Global recognition has enabled him to become a fashion icon who is sought after by advertisers to help promote their products.

- In November 2011 Beckham led LA Galaxy to victory over Houston Dynamo in the MLS Cup final, the championship match of major league soccer in the United States and Canada.

- In 2012 he confirmed his Ordinary Guy image by bringing out a range of male underwear for H&M.

By evoking one or two archetypes consistently throughout his career, David Beckham has used his talents to achieve an unusual level of commercial success.

Be selective about endorsements and recommendations

If you are well known, you may have opportunities to endorse products and services. If you choose them carefully, they can strengthen your brand as well as generating extra revenue. However, they must fit your brand image. Some Hollywood stars have appeared in advertisements for mundane products such as furniture that bear no relation to their brand and have thereby damaged it. By contrast, Nicole Kidman can only have enhanced her brand by appearing in the world's most expensive advertisement – for Chanel No. 5. This mini-film, directed by Baz Luhrmann, lasted nearly three minutes. Viewers commented afterwards on how beautiful she looked.

People in all walks of life make endorsements, sometimes without considering the effect on their brands. If a recruitment consultant asks you to suggest candidates, be wary of recommending a friend with a poor track record who is always looking for a new job. The recruiter may conclude that your judgement is also poor. It is better to help your friends directly than to misrepresent their abilities to others. Many recruitment consultants have a drop-down menu on their database so they can mark you down as a good or bad source. If they think you are good, you will be one of the first people they call about an exciting opportunity.

Chapter

22

Co-branding

Co-branding is when two or more brands join forces to bring a product or service to market. If their strengths complement each other, the end result will be far more powerful than anything they could have achieved on their own. They are sometimes described as *brand buddies.*

One example is the highly successful *Nike+*. These runners' shoes tell them via their iPod about their pace, the distance covered and the number of calories burned. The iPod also provides downloads of suitable running songs.

Co-branding can involve personal brands, too. Here are some examples:

- David Beckham joining Real Madrid, as described in the last chapter.
- Daniel Barenboim conducting any major orchestra.
- Oprah Winfrey interviewing other celebrities.

Co-branding also occurs when you work on a project with someone or join a company. Before you do so, it is worth considering the effect their brand will have on yours. You can take references. You can also talk to a few people informally without disclosing your plans. Everyone has their admirers and detractors, but common themes emerge quickly. If you are considering joining a company, you can track down people who used to work there and get their feedback. At least you will be going in with your eyes open. Do you feel comfortable being associated with them? How will it affect your brand? What are their values, as demonstrated by their behaviour?

We are not suggesting you work only with people who have the same talents or skills as you; it is usually better if those are different from your own. However, we do recommend working with people who have similar values. You are likely to agree on most things and spend far less time on management issues. You will also enjoy it and be more successful.

Think carefully before you add to your CV

Every move you make affects your brand, whether you are applying to a college or university, joining a company or starting a new one. Some people are so cautious that they never take a risk. Their CV lists one blue-chip name after another. However, the biggest successes often occur when this pattern is broken and someone goes beyond what is expected of them. For example, many successful entrepreneurs start their businesses just after losing a job.

Piggy-back on other people's brands

You can build your brand faster if your customers have strong brands that reflect well on you. Consumer brands are particularly good. People often think that the companies in question are much bigger than they really are.

John's first assignment after leaving Heidrick & Struggles was to recruit a finance director for Fitness First, Europe's leading health club chain. Although its revenues at the time were 'only' £100 million, it had a market capitalisation of £500 million and was a member of the FTSE Mid 250 Index. It was well known among people living or working in large cities. Fitness First is now the world's second-largest health club chain, with more than 1 million members. Its brand really helped to build John's brand as well as that of his new firm.

23

Building a team

Archetypes are very useful for building teams. Understanding your own archetype makes you more aware of those that other people evoke in their work. You can then choose colleagues who fit with you and the market you serve.

John and his colleagues were once asked to recruit a finance director for a large company that owns hundreds of pubs and is quoted on the London Stock Exchange. After visiting several pubs and meeting the board and management committee, John concluded that the organisation evoked the Ordinary Guy. The beer and food were of good quality but also affordable. The head office was open-plan and everyone ate in the same canteen. There was a minimum of hierarchy and they addressed each other by their first names.

The shortlist consisted of eight candidates, all of whom evoked the Ruler to a greater or lesser extent. They were all qualified accountants and had been finance director of a large division or an entire company. The board of directors wanted an element of the Ruler, to help keep hundreds of pubs under control and steadily expand the business.

Candidate A evoked only the Ruler. He had spent most of his career working in the head office of large companies. The board liked his financial control experience but felt he lacked any personal connection with their business.

Candidate B evoked both the Ruler and the Hero. He had been captain of the school rugby team and had nearly become an officer in the Royal Marines. Having trained as an accountant, he had specialised in tackling difficult projects and turning around failing companies. However, the board did not want the Hero. Their business had grown successfully over many years and they did not feel it needed rescuing.

The successful candidate evoked both the Ruler and the Ordinary Guy. He had attended an undistinguished school in a small industrial city. He had been one of very few pupils who had gone to university. He enjoyed spending time in pubs and the board felt he would fit their culture.

You can use archetypes to build *your* team. It may be that you and your colleagues evoke an archetype that reflects the underlying business. However, each member of the team can also evoke another archetype that reflects their particular role.

One example is an early-stage software company that evokes the Ruler. It helps companies to control their finances and manage risks. The chief executive is a former professional climber who does everything in a disciplined way. This evokes the Ruler and appeals to customers who wish to rule their business empires. He has a similar appeal among investors, who know that he is taking good care of their money. However, he also evokes the Magician, having bought the software from a liquidator in order to turn it into a viable business. The sales manager has a similarly disciplined approach. However, he also evokes the Ordinary Guy as he contacts potential customers and builds rapport with their staff at all levels.

Archetypes versus other models

You may be familiar with other psychological tools such as Myers–Briggs, which, like the archetypes described in this book, is based on the work of Carl Jung. The Myers–Briggs model measures personality styles on four dimensions that Jung described in his book, *Psychological Types,* published in 1920. In 1962, Isabel Myers and Kathryn Briggs published a questionnaire for identifying different kinds of personality: *The Myers–Briggs Type Indicator.* They used Jung's model, which they relabelled as follows:

E = Extravert or I = Introvert

S = Sensing or N = Intuition

T = Thinking or F = Feeling

J = Judging or P = Perceiving

If you take a Myers–Briggs test, it will measure you on each of these four axes. This can help you to understand how you communicate with other people, and how people can operate with styles that are very different from your own.

The essence of Myers–Briggs is that seemingly random variations in behaviour are in fact quite orderly and consistent. For example, someone who has a strong F orientation will find it easier to get along with a fellow F than with a strong T. You can also make sure there is a suitable balance of personalities in a team. For example, a strong P will tend to examine data continually, feeling more comfortable before a decision is made than when it has been made. By contrast, a strong J will want to get the job done and will feel more comfortable when a decision has been taken and implemented. In order to strike a balance between analysis and decisiveness, you need both types of personality in a team. The strong P will want to focus on the data, while the strong J will want to get the job done. Both are necessary for effective decision making.

How do archetypes fit with Myers–Briggs? The short answer is: with difficulty, even though many people have tried to make them fit. A more practical approach is to use each for a different purpose. They help to reveal different aspects of people.

In Chapter 9 we asked you to imagine yourself as a precious stone with many facets. It is for you to decide which facets you are going to show to the outside world at any particular time.

Exercise V: Other people's archetypes

Write down the names of people you work with closely. Which archetypes do they evoke consistently? If each evokes a different archetype, do they complement each other and make the team stronger? Do several of you evoke the same archetype? If so, would your team be stronger if it included people who evoked other archetypes?

....

....

....

....

....

Conclusion

The best way to market yourself is to build your personal brand. However, you have to know what you are selling. In other words, you have to know yourself. For most of us, this is a lifelong voyage of discovery.

We hope you have found the exercises helpful. If you have skipped any, we strongly encourage you to go back and fill in the gaps. Discovering yourself is the most powerful way to learn; we have provided a framework to help you do so.

Here is a checklist to make sure you have completed the key steps:

- Identify your talents.
- Identify your values.
- Identify your unique combination of talents, skills and experiences.
- Develop a sense of purpose by clarifying your mission.
- Decide which archetype (or two) you are going to evoke consistently.
- Make sure your CV conveys your purpose and fits your market.
- Summarise what you do in three seconds.
- Make sure that what you say and do evokes your main archetype.
- Remain in the present. Accept things as they are.
- Work out the ZOPA before you negotiate your remuneration.
- Become more visible, using the appropriate technology.
- Focus on serving people rather than trying to get something from them.

- Offer to help people whose work you admire.

- Manage your contacts on your computer and/or smartphone.

- Use social media to maintain and expand your network.

- Protect your brand and consider extending it.

- If you can, piggy-back on other people's brands.

- Use archetypes to build a strong team around you.

If you complete each of these steps you will build a strong brand and be memorable. The effects are frequently dramatic. The appendix that follows provides four case studies.

We look forward to hearing your story, and wish you every success!

John Purkiss and **David Royston-Lee**

www.johnpurkiss.com and www.davidroystonlee.com

Appendix: Case studies

The following case studies are based on our experience of advising clients. They have been altered to protect the clients' identities. We hope these examples will give you some ideas for building your own brand.

The Information Technologist

David Royston-Lee met Paul while speaking at an international conference. Paul followed David's recommendation to read *Brand You* and then contacted him for further assistance.

During their first meeting David realised that Paul was so busy at work that he had no time to concentrate on anything else. His first attempt at the exercises in *Brand You* was patchy. However, Paul had recently married and was expecting his first child. He now wanted to make rapid progress in his career. Like most people, he had had no real training in how to manage his life or his career.

Paul was an expert in a particular software application. He had developed a reputation for going beyond the call of duty on behalf of clients, and had won awards for customer service. However, Paul had not been promoted for five years. Going through the exercises in *Brand You*, he quickly realised he had been his own worst enemy as far as promotion was concerned. He had concentrated on doing a good job and had kept his head down for far too long. While focusing on what other people wanted from him, he had lost sight of what *he* wanted from his role.

While analysing his talents (Exercise A), Paul realised that he loved working directly with clients. He wondered how he might be able to move from IT support into a sales role. When he looked at his talents in relation to his values, he identified a clear theme, which involved solving complex problems in challenging situations. This gradually emerged as one of the key elements in his mission.

Over the next few months he clarified the talents he wanted to use and asked several people he respected how they saw him. In terms of the archetypes, he identified with the Ordinary Guy and the Magician. His colleagues and clients said they saw both archetypes in him. Being very similar to his clients, he understood their situations. He was often able to produce amazingly simple solutions to their problems, as if by magic.

The coaching sessions improved Paul's confidence, based on his awareness of his talents and the way he used them. As is so often the case, once Paul changed, the world around him changed, too. A vacancy arose in his company for a sales person specialising in his particular area. Although he had no sales experience, he was now able to talk about himself with confidence and had the support of his colleagues, so the company gave him a chance. He loves his new role and achieved his first-year sales target of £1 million after only six months.

The Entrepreneur

Jessica had worked in human resources (HR) for more than 15 years and was an HR director with a large, international company. When she gained a new boss with an unhelpful attitude towards women in senior roles she decided to agree a redundancy package and explore other options, which she had been considering doing for a while. A friend gave Jessica a copy of *Brand You* and she contacted the authors to see whether they could help. She decided on a programme of eight sessions with David to redefine her working life.

Although Jessica knew herself well, she approached the exercises as though she were starting from scratch. She wanted to conduct a complete audit of her talents and values, and develop a network of contacts that extended beyond HR and large companies.

Jessica explored new opportunities and started learning the cello, as she had always wanted. She also spoke to people in the markets for accessories and affordable art.

One theme that emerged from the exercises was her ability to throw herself into new situations. She realised that this had been missing from her HR roles in the last five years. She loved taking risks, provided they were measured ones, as she had an eye for detail and was quite analytical in her thinking.

Jessica understood that the combination of the Ruler and the Hero suited her well. She was organised and cautious, but also prepared to take risks and be noticed.

Within four sessions Jessica had decided to explore self-employment. She began to talk to her contacts around the world, to obtain samples of accessories that she could potentially sell in the UK. She also talked to some of David's previous clients to understand the potential pitfalls in this kind of venture. Although she was careful, Jessica took the risk of setting up her own business at a time when many others were closing down. However, she had done her homework and identified good suppliers in Asia for silks and in South America for silver.

Jessica is succeeding in a difficult market. She is also enjoying her work.

The Investment Manager

Peter had worked in investment since graduation. He was now a successful manager of a large, international equity portfolio, and was planning to launch a new fund. Peter read Brand You and then contacted John Purkiss for some individual help. He realised that he needed a stronger personal brand, both to maintain the support he required within his organisation and to attract new investors.

Although Peter spoke at investment conferences and was often in the press, he did not stand out from his peer group. John reviewed the recent press coverage and concluded that most investment managers in Peter's sector evoked the Sage. They talked about the economy, the state of the financial markets, etc. in a similarly knowledgeable fashion. John also interviewed some of Peter's colleagues, professional advisers and clients. They saw a wide range of archetypes in him, which suggested that his brand was not clearly defined.

John asked Peter to complete the talents, values, mission, purpose and archetypes exercises. They agreed that Peter would look at all aspects of his life, not just his work.

It turned out that many of the high points in Peter's life had involved working in a small team, succeeding against the odds. In his youth Peter had been a mountaineer. Now his passion was yacht racing. His preferred investment style was special situations. He liked to back companies that had fallen from favour but could storm back to victory under the right conditions. In some cases Peter helped to create those conditions by ousting an underperforming chief executive or pushing a company's board to make other radical changes.

It became clear to both of them that Peter's preferred archetype was the Hero, which he evoked alongside the Sage so clients would continue to rely on his expert knowledge of the markets. They were prepared to take measured risks, without being reckless.

Peter and John explored ways in which he could evoke the Hero archetype consistently to increase his profile, both internally and externally. Peter decided to use social networking sites to extend his reach and promote his brand. He began by opening a Twitter account, in his own name for future use. That took five minutes.

He then 'followed' the journalists who had interviewed him recently, so he could keep up to date with what they were thinking and writing, via his smartphone.

Working on his personal brand has energised Peter in many ways. His boss and immediate colleagues have noticed a difference in terms of his confidence and awareness of his clients' needs.

Peter has also decided to get some coaching in storytelling. Rather than bombard people with statistics, he will use concise stories that evoke the Hero and the Sage.

The Yoga Teacher

Michelle had been teaching yoga for some time. However, she realised she needed to re-evaluate both her life and her commitment to yoga as she was finding it increasingly difficult to strike a balance. She worked hard but did not earn much money. She often 'over-served' her clients, leaving little time for herself and neglecting her own needs. Once she and her friends had completed David's archetype questionnaire, it was no surprise to discover that she evoked the Caregiver.

Michelle realised that she needed to develop her business so that she was not the only one teaching individuals and running workshops. She simply did not have time to do everything.

Looking back on her life, Michelle realised that she had experienced many high points during her earlier career as a nurse. She also had a long-term interest in nutrition. Both these factors differentiated her from other yoga teachers.

Michelle found it hard to break her addiction to doing everything herself, but has now begun to work with others and develop her brand through social media. She also gives talks on integrating yoga with diet, something she would not have contemplated a few months ago. She admits money is still tight but she can see a way forward. By working with colleagues who have similar values, she can build a much stronger client base and earn a more consistent income.

Recommended reading

It's Not How Good You Are, It's How Good You Want To Be, by Paul Arden (Phaidon Press, 2003)

The Crystal-Barkley Guide to Taking Charge of Your Career, by Nella Barkley and Eric Sandburg (Workman Publishing, 1996)

Raving Fans: A Revolutionary Approach to Customer Service, by Ken Blanchard and Sheldon Bowles (HarperCollins Business, 1998)

Wholeness and the Implicate Order, by David Bohm (Routledge Classics, 2002)

Screw It, Let's Do It, by Richard Branson (Virgin Books, 2006)

Flow – The Classic Work on How to Achieve Happiness, by Mihaly Csikszentmihalyi (Rider & Co, revised edition 2002)

Lateral Thinking, by Edward De Bono (Penguin, 2009)

Getting to Yes: Negotiating Agreement Without Giving In, by Roger Fisher, William Ury and Bruce Patton (Random House Business Books, revised second edition 2003)

Tribes: We Need You to Lead Us, by Seth Godin (Piatkus, 2008)

The Storytelling Pocketbook, by Roger E. Jones (Management Pocketbooks, 2012)

Search Engine Optimization for Dummies, by Peter Kent (John Wiley & Sons, fourth edition 2010)

Metaphors We Live By, by George Lakoff and Mark Johnson (University of Chicago Press, 2003)

The Tao of Coaching, by Max Landsberg (Profile Books, new edition 2003)

Warren Buffett Speaks – Wit and Wisdom from the World's Greatest Investor, by Janet Lowe (John Wiley & Sons, second edition 2007)

The Writer's Journey – From Inspiration to Publication, by Julia McCutchen (Firefly Media, 2004)

The Hero and the Outlaw – Building Extraordinary Brands Through the Power of Archetypes, by Margaret Mark and Carol S. Pearson (McGraw-Hill Professional, 2001)

Follow Your Heart: Finding Purpose in Your Life and Work, by Andrew Matthews (Seashell Books, 1997)

Brand It Like Beckham – The Story of How Brand Beckham Was Built, by Andy Milligan (Cyan Books, 2004)

The Minto Pyramid Principle: Logic in Writing, Thinking and Problem Solving, by Barbara Minto (1996 edition, available from www.barbaraminto.com)

The Pyramid Principle: Logic in Writing and Thinking, by Barbara Minto (Financial Times/Prentice Hall, third edition 2008)

Ogilvy on Advertising, by David Ogilvy (Prion Books, new edition 2007)

Confessions of an Advertising Man, by David Ogilvy (Southbank Publishing, 2011)

Managing Your Self: Management by Detached Involvement, by Jagdish Parikh (Wiley-Blackwell, new edition 1993)

Ken Purkiss – 50 Photos, by John Purkiss and Robert Coggins (Kensworth Press, 2007)

How to be Headhunted, by John Purkiss & Barbara Edlmair (How To Books, 2005)

Are You Ready To Succeed? – Unconventional Strategies for Achieving Personal Mastery in Business and in Life, by Srikumar Rao (Rider & Co, 2007)

The Element: How Finding Your Passion Changes Everything, by Ken Robinson and Lou Aronica (Penguin, 2010)

How to Become an Icon, by Simon Silvester (Executive Planning Director, Young & Rubicam: http://emea.yr.com/icon.pdf)

Screw Work, Let's Play, by John Williams (Prentice Hall, 2010)

What did you think of this book?

We're really keen to hear from you about this book, so that we can make our publishing even better.

Please log on to the following website and leave us your feedback.

It will only take a few minutes and your thoughts are invaluable to us.

www.pearsoned.co.uk/bookfeedback

Archetypes

For your convenience, here is a summary of the archetypes:

The Caregiver	Helps and protects from harm
The Creator	Compelled to create and innovate
The Explorer	Explores and discovers
The Hero	Acts courageously to put things right
The Innocent	Seeks purity, goodness and happiness
The Jester	Has a good time but may convey a serious message
The Lover	Finds and gives love and sensual pleasure
The Magician	Transforms situations
The Ordinary Guy/Girl	OK as they are; connects with others
The Outlaw	Rebels and breaks the rules
The Ruler	Takes control; creates order out of chaos
The Sage	Helps people to understand their world

Please visit www.brandyou.info for the latest information on personal branding.

Index